Blob Mentality

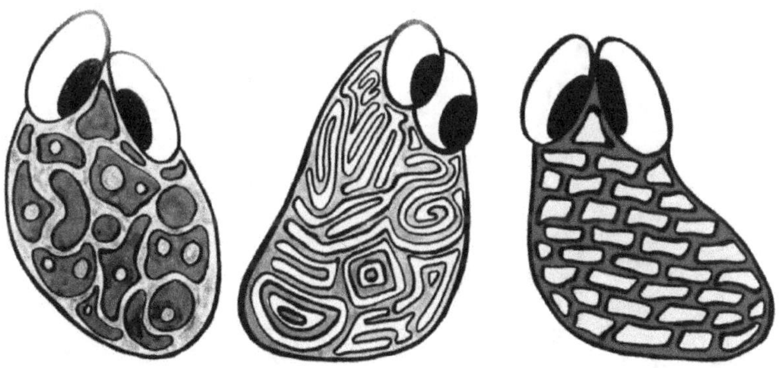

by Refried Bean

Blob Mentality

**in memory of Catherine Polit,
Sarah Braud, Raewyn and Daniel,
Linda, and all the victims of
microwaves, pottery glaze, and splenda.**

Legal Notice

This book is really three books combined, with some original posts and drawings left out because of printing limitations and decisions to show mercy to some bad people. But I do say some stuff about some of the oppression that was hurting me at the time of writing this book, as well as including some very accurate recollections of the work history that left me dependent on people who thankfully were in the habit of helping people like me but who did not share some of my missions that might have prevented a lot of societal problems. Is it really a lack or support, and a "nonfamation" case for Judgement Day like I have suspected, or is it something more calculated and offensive? Probably both, I don't know. That is part of the wrenching depicted in some of these blog posts that are in fact a bit much, but a sincere reaction, too, to some kind of finale of people conveying their personal hatred towards me, and choosing their politics over kindness after a very dramatic effort from me to really get along with anyone and even consider the cumulative accusations against me and others from my religion, to wonder if we were the ones who always chose an agenda, and to try to work with people as if they weren't the two dimensional villains that their actions seemed to suggest. But instead I was faced with an abuse completeness once again, a totality of squelching that I am familiar with and know where it comes from. It is Satanic, and always has been, since the beginning of middle school when I decided to follow Jesus Christ and found a creeping guilt manipulation and unexpected opposition to my efforts at serving others in the most basic meaningful ways. There were people who seemed to think that I should not be allowed to be good until they were too, and then decided that it was more fun to prevent my goodness than to achieve their own service to others. To think it was just a personal situation and get through it only to find a larger politics that matches it has been surprising to the point where I haven't believed it on some levels and have ended up trusting people who maybe I should not have trusted. I think God favors the naivete in cases like that and his disgust at people's arrogant control freak power plays will be revealed in awesome totality sooner than we realize. People have told themselves that no one will know if half the people aren't working, or if they just help themself to someone else's harvest, or if they just go ahead and choose the racism because some identities are in season with the media. Is it stupider to think that half the country won't know what's true, or to think that God himself doesn't know. Well some of these people believe they are God themselves, so maybe that is part of the problem.

Anyway, I am finishing this introduction and publishing this book with a realistic expectation that it could also be silenced in printed form similar to these past ten years where I should have been successful and published like many of the people who have hurt me. Tell yourself it is not true, or that I deserved to be destroyed based on history, or privilege, or association with the person you really hate who is Jesus Christ. But it is exactly that tiny fear or slight objection that will probably eventually catch fire to burn away the rest of your ignorance. That is what I have prayed for in my years of staying alive like a fool. I will still advocate for others to do the same, though you can see in these posts how that determination has eroded. It has created a form of law school for me, so I can show up on Judgement Day and help defend almost anyone now that I have found patience for the people of recent evil days.

a special commendation to Petco
who provided such shockingly reliable pet food
without any lapse whatsoever during Covid

acknowledgements

thank you so much to

Ellen and Michelle, Tony Sorrow, Angel, Mark, from NAMI
David, Tiffany, Robyn, Drena, Dr. Nadkarni, Pam and Karen, Joe
Sally, Razneet, Adeera, Adelyn, and Parris, from Pathway to Home
Joy, Allison, Diana, Ryan, Claire, Jenny, Jane, Victorio, Paragraph
Jillian, Mo, Lucien, Dr. Garvin, Di Fan, Jennifer, Jason, from NYP
Dr. Chou, Dr. Raisin, and Dr. Ubaktu, Dr. Lee, Dr. Li, MSUC, 34th
precinct cops, Dr. Pou, Dr. Ramada, Estelita, Judith P, Dr. Rojas,
Tres, Valentina, Heights Physicians Group, Sevani, Sophfronia,
Carla, Antoinetta C, Quora, Christina B., Venancio, Rev Dr. Heber
Brown, Nate Stuckey, Delvonna, Candace, Sandra, Sushama Austin-
Connor, Gloria, Ann, Melvin, Bernice, Denise, Forever Coffee, Bait
and Hook, Beth, Haley, Katherine, Wendy, Catherine, Amanda,
Krystn, Heather, Johelis, Nieve, George, Blad, Fire, Robert, Scott,
Starbucks and Subway, Tommy, Bin, Stella, Jeromie, Craig, Gayle,
Jill, David, Mike, Margaret Foster, Leslie, TCG, Louise, Rachel,
Melissa, Melissa, Crystal, Jericho, VCFA, Daniel, Raewyn, Nathan,
Melissa, Franklyn, Maribel, Frank from Animal Control, Way to go
and thanks, Sasha, Malia, Bo, GT, RG, TNC, AJK, and millenials.

Anne, Mom, and Dad
Presbyterians
Catholics
Jewish friends

also, belated acknowledgements for Forgiveness Flag:
thank you so much, Kathleen Graber, Jody Gladding,
Matthew Dickman, Claire Bateman, and Kimberly Simms

Thanks also again to the whole conspiracy.
I have not done well with being tortured
and I am sorry I cursed too much and was bad.

added list for thanks

More barnes and noble

School and Greenville

Kiersten, romi, starbucks people again.

Oprah winfrey, ellen degeneres

Hilary price, m.c. carpenter, music people

Food people names food network people names

Petco

Dolly Parton

Bobbi

Vera

Dr Erica

Kelly Harwood

John, Tia, Jeff

Drena

Tonnie's Cupcakes of Inwood

more acknowledgements: dr ying, dr frissora, dr rao, AOC, Whitey, Will, Maria AB., patricia, barbara, jacqueline, bashqueda, dr Lin, dr Bismati, jordan, pr reminiscient, erica, erica, dr havarti, dr luciano, dr. hirsch, Dr. Billakota, Maria from Paragraph, Will, Mihee, add name from write-up, mystery people bonus pending, Panda House, Novel Retreat People, Riley, Crystal, Adam, Nils, Elizabeth, Kath, Robin, Michiah, Frank, Ellen, Rashmi, Chanel, Wayne, Becky, Connie, Sheila, Dahlma, Nerissa, Jim, Su, Regina, Dr. Harding, Dr. Heravian, Dr. Kuo, Dr. Ouyang, Dr. Kenny, Dr. Williams, Dot, Lynnae, Tony, John B, Eva D, Lyle, Theresa, Aesha, Jaylema, Jean, Rodolpho, Eric, Dan, Precious, Jesse, Ian, Kerem, Mike, Michelle, Katie, Kesionna, Rondall, Devon, Rhonda, Alex, Pam, Lynn, Pace, Sarah, Jessica, Anthony, Peerfessionals, Power Peers, Humble Bs, I miss you gice already, Alan S, John W, Amy E, Susannah, Amy IG friend and family, Mark, Susan, Susan R, Susan boll weevil friend, Alicia, Anndrea, Cecil, Tammy, Lisa, David, Mrs. Poster, BJT, Hamlet helper, Annette, Jenny S, Emily S, Denny, Jared, Catherine and Mitchell, Gwen and Brad Martin, Kristiana and Todd, Mary, Mary, Marquavius, Cocoa, Nigel, Suave, Jyrek, Kianna, Junior, Tamia, Tyrek, Juju, TJ, Dreke, Monnie, Marissa, Jessie, Elizabeth, the Mexicans, facebook kids, Linda Tassie, Youthbase, Mental Health America, Frazee Center, Safe Harbor, Trinity Lutheran, St. Elizabeth the New Martyr, St. John, Our Lady Queen of Martyrs, Iglesias Church, Ft. George Collegiate, Rita, Maryam, Adam, Cyndi, Umberto, thank you so much, domino guardians, Kismat Indian Cuisine, Refried Beans Mexican Restaurant, Pizza Cake, MTA.

Autism and the God who sees
By Refried Bean, LMSW

I had an idea this morning for an academic theology paper on the way autism eye contact problems relate to the famous presbyterian theology of God having to look away from his suffering son on the cross, only to then see the now reconcilable humans who were alienated because of sin. It is foundational theology that some ministers keep to themselves as they tell people the simple gospel of salvation through faith in Christ. But the theology of God overlooking sin goes as deep or deeper than our real-life problems, and it can actually be a challenge to understand.

The concept is basically that forgiveness is really a matter of overlooking error, but human sin is collectively and individually so bad that to overlook it, God has to look away from us in complete disgust. But because of his son Jesus who became human, God can still look at people in that "moment" and view anyone with complete unwavering love.

This theology sometimes comes across as the opposite of what it means, like when people say, God doesn't see you as you are; he sees you as you should be or will be some day. It is so confusing, like okay, God can't see me but loves me anyway? So his love is based on nothing instead of something? That is messed up, and the opposite of how it really is.

Anyway, my idea for a paper was to consider this concept alongside the eye contact symptoms of autism spectrum disorder. Avoiding eye contact is a hallmark of autism and aspergers, and I have a suspicion that the most technical neurological explanation of it all by itself would hold within it some of the most extreme and profound theology involving God's gaze upon his creation, our varied responses to it, and interestingly, the challenge presented to almost our whole society of how to care for people with autism in light of Christianity, or for many of us, how to love God while being autistic in this life.

But as I think of it, a more personal essay comes to mind, lighter, maybe, but with lifelong suffering and family problems creating a dear cost behind these ideas. It is reminiscent of God's priceless provision of his son, and yet fractionally infinitesimal, as anything in this life becomes when set before the power of God's cross.

When I was younger, I remember my mom complaining to me that I did not make eye contact, sometimes suggesting that I was dishonest or "defiant" because of it. But a lot of my indirectness with her, which eventually became a slight tendency to lie, was a reaction to her own autism symptom, which was a constant obsession with me and monitoring of every mood and facial expression I experienced. She was ashamed of my gender problem, which I was mostly unaware of, and she could not look away as she did everything she could to control me to be normal. It is still not over even though I am 43 years old. In fact, she just picked me up from the mall and told me to sit in a room with dad more even though he is not talking to me.

Trauma and humiliation have made my autism symptoms worse now than when I was a kid, when some of it was useful in helping me be funny and successful. The tendency towards indirectness was part of my writing talent, and I learned to tell the truth as bravely as I could after the holy spirit helped me realize that I needed to be a more honest person. I still work hard to tell the truth and have no patience with people who commonly see eye contact problems as an indication of dishonesty.

I have a twin sister, too, who got neglected some as I absorbed too much attention as a kid, and our family problems became something I have been trying to work out in my mind for my whole adult life. I just haven't understood what went wrong, why it seems like my sister is still mad at me because I did what I was supposed to in middle school and high school, and why my dad did not intervene to help me escape from my mom. And the most baffling thing is something that drove me towards Catholicism in my mind, which is a sense that these people really did have some dirt on me, and there was some spiritual authority I did not have as an evangelical because of some failure to share my faith with them, even though they were also Presbyterians and went to the same church as me. I actually still don't know if there are some kind of principalities behind them, holding hundreds or even thousands of potential converts hostage as my determination to share my faith has been perpetually unsuccessful and thwarted by people's ongoing hatred of me, often seeming to be related to my not having a family of my own, or my decision to try not to be gay. Everything I do is wrong, everywhere I go. I have three masters degrees and my average income for the past 20 years amounts to about 12 thousand dollars a year. Even some of that is partially because of recent years on ssdi after being abused to the point of disability at my retail job, already many steps down from an advertising career that I would have been more than capable of. Meanwhile, my parents continue to pay me not to be gay through loan money. This is the autistic life, with a soundtrack of more and more inappropriate music playing in retail stores as the rest of our culture overcompensates for their own shame of feeling gay. There is something in the water, but no one will address it because the people who figured out that it is better to go ahead and be yourself enjoy too much being able to shame the evangelicals who thought maybe they should pretend to be the way they think God originally designed people.

Anyway, that denial, especially in the south, is another "looking away" theme. It is interesting, because I feel like I can see a looking away that happens from not caring, and a different, more forgivable looking away that comes from caring so much that you truly can't bear it. It is the theme of that southern dixie song, which is relevant in a similar way.

I think some of my confusion about how spiritual authority works started in college after I became a Young Life leader, which was a Christian ministry for high school kids. They taught us that it was good to "win the right to be heard," as we provided clubs and bible studies to help high school students just a little bit younger than us learn about Jesus Christ. But I did not have a good experience. I got over the difficult social hurdle of starting off as a leader and getting to know kids at the high school, but only gave one talk and found myself instead being in social challenge after social challenge, never getting to actually share my faith, and instead feeling an increased sense of rejection that I did not even experience myself in high school. I think a lot of it had to do with Young Life's hyper-gendered strategies to win over kids' trust, which for me made there be too much of the world's poison mixed in with the bait. I ended up feeling more at home with college friends who openly rejected Christianity. I think that is all part of the challenge that our whole country has had to navigate, and there is no need for me to let it ruin my whole life. However, there was something else about it all that drove me towards concluding that my role was to be a humiliated and rejected Catholic monk in a bookstore instead of a successful and loved evangelical in a church. And it had to do with my family. I just feel like people knew something was wrong in my family, and they honored my family's grudges against me. And it confuses me to try to figure out for my whole life if God was also mad. I just don't understand. If my authority was too compromised by not helping my family enough with their religion, then doesn't that make the Young Life people wrong about the message they are not letting me tell everyone? It's so confusing. Did the protestants not force me to be a failed Catholic priest? For everyone else's treatment of me, I am supposed to view everything as God's plan, but for my own behavior, it is all up to me and I have to be a Catholic saint. Well I have delivered on that, thanks to the miracle of God's love at the cross, which seems much more powerful and immanent than part of a map of predestined history. And yet Jesus did say "it is finished."

When I took a theology class a few years ago, I finally "saw" the theology I had heard before, and felt that previous explanations of Jesus dying instead of me weren't as accurate as maybe seeing that Jesus died "as me," and that is why it could count as being instead of me. It is more than just a word game language stumble, and I received a supernatural baptism of the holy spirit in those days that I finally was able to believe from seeing.

And now what can I do for other people? I still do not know. A lot of autistic people love animals, and I think partly it is because it is a way that we can experience love in a more indirect way that does not cause us to have to avert our eyes from the intense gaze of people who we either do want attention from or don't want attention from. It kind of becomes comical to think of how many times a day the looking and not looking topic plays out in our lives. I think a lot of autistic people could really have a special appreciation for how God approached us through Christ, causing love to be possible after all, and inviting us to behold an innocent lamb who takes away the sins of the world. A grieving, bullied friend being mocked and slaughtered on our behalf in order to allow all the time in the world to untangle the neverending social webs of compromised living from a society that refused to let us be ourselves and then punished us for it.

I am so thankful for the miracle of being a Presbyterian after all, or before all, even though I am happy to share a Catholic rendition of the looking and overlooking theology, which is simply the opposite of what the Presbyterians say. Instead of God having to look away from his suffering son, couldn't you say instead that in those six hours of the crucifixion, God did look at his son, viewing the horrific spectacle in order to give everyone else a chance to adjust our reactions while he counts to three and allows time for anyone to change their mockery to silence, and then to appreciation, and finally to worship, for eternity.

wrangle and defangle.

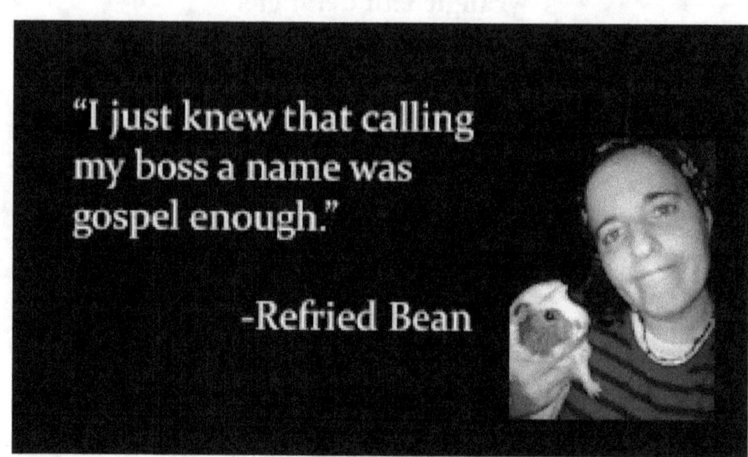

"I just knew that calling my boss a name was gospel enough."

-Refried Bean

Inaugural Poem II

Obama is my favorite president.
i think they should rename Alabama
Alobama.

obama gave us a health care bill
the other presidents just made us ill.

abraham lincoln wasnt that bad.
james madison did not make me too mad.

but some presidents say words like pre-existing conditions,
when really the goal should have been reparitions

That is why I am voting for bernie
to take all the cash that the rich people earnie.

poem

gastritis

gastritis

why do i have gastritis

it's not that bad

it's not a fad

I got to ride in an ambulance.

poem

what if you ran 80 miles

and then saw

that the finish line

was a wall of flame

Killer Comedy and the Comedy Killer

Francisco was a comedian in the very populated metro region of the south north quadrant. His shows had been getting more consistent, and he had a steady income from selling CDs and teaching some workshops. Most of his jokes were about dating, and office work, or funny things about relatives and awkward conversations. One night, in the middle of a show, he suddenly thought of a new joke and just blurted it out with no planning.

"What if someone was born with clothes on?" he said, standing at the mike while the audience roared laughing. The joke's appreciative reception was as unexpected as the joke itself. Francisco started riffing on it, creating a wave of humor for the laughter to surf on. "It's like, okay, do you wash the clothes on the baby, or what. Like is the baby just supposed to always have clothes on?" One guy in the middle of the comedy club was laughing harder than everyone. Francisco continued. "And do you tell people? Like if they say what a cute outfit, do you say, "thanks, it's from that store downtown, called Miracle Baby." Francisco kept thinking of more to say. "Wouldn't you feel guilty if you had a baby shower and some people would like know that the baby already had an outfit, like the muppets, like Ernie and Bert who wear the same shirt every day?"

The guy laughing so hard in the middle of the crowd could not stop laughing. He was keeled over, clutching his stomach, drooling. His girlfriend next to him slowed her laughing and started to look concerned. A few other people nearby also seemed in distress, but mostly able to calm down. Francisco saw him but decided to go for one final punch. "It's like, okay, so much for hand me downs, you know?"

This is when the drooling guy fell off his chair, and was suddenly motionless. He had died laughing. Some people came to his side and tried to call for medical attention. Many people still could not control themselves laughing and just left the comedy club.

Francisco watched from the stage, started to feel an odd feeling of pride, with some serious bafflement, but then smirked to himself, left the stage, and sat in a back room feeling a sense of power that he felt he had waited for all his life. "I was born for this," he thought to himself, laughing, hesitating to make sure he would not die from his own joke, and then leaving to go home.

The joke became part of his routine, and because he toured all around from city to city, people didn't realize there was a pattern happening when someone would die at every show.

"I'm a freakin' serial killer," thought Francisco, and then wondered if he could work that idea into the routine some.

Finally, at one of the shows as Francisco started talking about what kind of outfit a kid could be born in, like would it have a whale on the pocket or do you make the kid keep wearing the hat and socks or not, people started to lose control like usual. But a heckler stood up and started giving Francisco trouble. "Hey man, what we are wondering is what kind of outfit you're going to jail in," said the guy standing up. Some FBI agents then came on stage and took Francisco to the station for questioning. The heckler walked up behind the microphone and said, "This isn't funny to me. I was born with clothes on."

List of Visions

It seems to be temporal lobe epilepsy with hypergraphia and
memory loss. Here are some of the recent visions. I think sometimes
I see the stuff after feeling some love from my true church
background that was kept away from me for many years and could
not be replaced by anything else including other churches.

a snake like an eel on sand and gravel
a snake with a flickering black tongue
a dead white guy with a sagging face and hollowed out eyes
a flat guy behind me on an operating table with a white and black
speckled face and a scar down his eye like the Kiss rock stars and
scar from the lion king with streaks of blond hair
a branch with ice melting
Daniel from the Bible
a cat in the other room
a small skull
someone who looks like Tina Turner
a commencement speaker in a purple and black robe who reminds
me of someone from a movie
a young chinese female speaking casually at a government podium
some other faces that show up and fade
a midget with a lot of make-up in front of NYU hospital
a blue lady with brown curly hair coming out of someone
near Bellevue
a guy with white plastic eyes standing next to my bed for two days
a guy with a beard who comes out of a mexican kid
and starts to attack me
Jesus Christ and then another Jesus Christ who seems bad and the
good Jesus shoots the bad Jesus and travels to Barnes and Noble in
Greenville to play games
a close up of grayish green smooth snakes
a powdery white faced bald guy in a poster of new york city
barking orders
a short bald scary red guy right in front of me

an scraggly old white man in the distance
E.T. but he looks younger
Saddam Hussein looking younger
a cup of coffee with Reeses pieces dropped into it
a black flappy thing flying across my room
in a dream, leaving a racism lecture with Connie May Fowler and
we are in a stone courtyard of a church or Abbey and there is a
statue of Mary probably holding Jesus in a ledge indentation but it is
really Mary and not made of stone
I see a bowl of white slate like a mountain on the campus of
Princeton Seminary and there is a fine brown dust on the rocks in
retrospect but it is a brighter white than happens on this earth and it
has to do with justice
a tiny vision of Jesus's face on the speckled floor tiles of NY
Presbyterian ER.
a scene at my grandmother's house where I am digging hairballs out
of the floorboards and having Christmas discussions with my sister
and other people and Jesus makes a joke about buying a blue book
from Barnes and Noble
a voice in an empty gray space saying "Nellie" really loudly
a dead body holding a human head next to me when I wake up in a
tomb during sleep paralysis
a dream about someone from my life helping me but there are two
bad things chasing us and I tell one to ask Jesus Christ for help and
when I say "do you remember him," the bad spirit says it at the same
time through my mouth as I wake up and feel relieved
but the other one gets away
an African American lady with dreadlocks checking on me near my
bed and a Dominican lady in the other room.
a black lady waiting outside the door of apartments on another floor
a verve that flies me up in the sky and I look down and see a
sacrificial altar area on a New York garden roof like a European
garden or Inca temple or one of those scary stone slabs
in Lord of the Rings

two dreams where there is another apartment system overlapping
this apartment in another realm and I go upstairs and people are
partying in other rooms and I don't know if it is good or bad
a girl like an incubus pressing down on my chest trying to keep me
from breathing during a sleep paralysis where I say you need to ask
Jesus Christ for help and she looks hopeful
and leaves out the window.
in a dream someone near a lake at a camp talking to someone else
and then abuses me in my room as a tactile hallucination
a dream about Jacqui where she is the principal at a high school
where I was teaching and did not do well but then quit because of
the bag of syrup and felt better
a dream where DBB falls from the ladder at the mall near two
enemies and I call 911
a dream where I am helping Dayle in a headquarters that gets nuked
from nearby and I look out for a toddler as my arms become
glowingly translucent as an X ray
a dream where I am at a reunion for the ministry I could not do and I
see that it has to do with my mom being treated bad in her life
a dream where I see the risen selves of two people I know in heaven
and I can't play hide and seek because of trauma
a dream where I see Fred Turner at a camp but it is his earth self
and not risen self
a movie on the side of a building in NYC that is a muppet movie
scene where Jack the muppet breaks through the screen except he is
really Jesus Christ dying for our sins

I think I should not always call stuff demons but I think that a lot of
it is actually the illumination of misportrayals that are meant to
either tempt, accuse, or deceive.

The most extreme spells were after walking about ten miles on a hot
day and I was able to interpret secret messages from God in a coded
literary way like reading symbolism and initials for about four hours
or more and then had to say okay that is enough and was in a trance
for a day or so until taking some risperdal.

I think a demon named Macifer has been torturing my family for many years and I thought a few years ago that it was over and a whole civilization had been freed but I am not sure. I do not really know what I am supposed to do. I think that the people who are torturing me for supposedly benevolent reasons are wrong.

What is the Problem

I'm very rude to America
even though America
hasn't been that rude to me
except for the subway ads
and bad music.
There are freight trains of thought
and roller coasters of thought.
There are Cassandra Crossing movies
about a virus on trains
and that is why we play the piano
on a Tuesday morning
for volunteer work
and a golden coin
from who?
Possibly from Moses
or a cartoon cow
who says moo when you
tell him your problem.
This poem will probably
fix everything
if people read it plus
fix everything.

"Don't argue with God's decretive will."

Something I have always found crazy
is how there aren't many potpourri scents
called "electrical fire."

nami prompt

something i feel compelled to hide is mexicans in a basement to
keep them safe from the bad people. well people are saying that
really you have friends in a basement to be nice to which is your
apartment super and you were supposed to take out the trash today
and it was the one thing you knew you were supposed to do for the
day besides talk to the church person and drink coffee and instead
you cooked with the worchester sauce you knew was questionable.

so now the h pylori results are no longer reliable

and you have triple crimes against all the people
who were nice to you

and three sad or mad facial expressions to interpret
with hours of worry.

what have we learned

we have learned something about people being mean to me and then
it turns out they were plenty nice except i think they weren't and
people messed up my peer counseling application on purpose.

it was razneet, peer cert board, tami and dianna, rita and maryam,
mark zuckerberg, dr nadkarni, dr. luciano, maya, and frank from
pest control.

interpretations

i communicated with someone from my past which is the mystery person who contacted me through a training video. the title said do you still like me. and then the video was a creepy housing online video of an apartment tenant morphing into different identities and i told the people on the survey that i liked that video and thought it was cool.

so i guess that is that unless the person was rude with that bad person from our class who lost me as a friend for everyone and now they will be remembered like the purple and black robe demon whose profile reminded me of a certain movie.

i saw it after reading an essay and that person should get a commendation beyond the prophecy about china that i can't share because millions of people could die.

The Creed of Mental Illness Church

the surprise is that dianna and tami tried to kill me.

but really it was the peer academy people trying to trigger a seizure
in front of the microscopic videos flying all around us that are
recording footage to be spliced and used to frame us for all the
crimes in the world.

on judgement day when people watch the evidence against them
they will think it is all over but what it will really mean is that
everyone's schizophrenia diagnosis has to be revoked and all former
mental patients are found guilty of malingering and sent to a jail
without walls where there is pizza and ice cream for everyone every
day for eternity.

New Years Resolutions

i have a problem wasting food
and doing bad too much.
I waste the cheese and then the cream
and then the such and such.

but there is proof that i am not
as bad as it all sounds
i can't have wasted everything
to be 200 pounds.

The History of Ultimate Galactic Wars

I am going to reach for the stars with this poem.
The literal stars in recently discovered galaxy G657,
a spiral galaxy with blue and bright nebulas,
which also have some planets.
On one of the planets
a nice being named Sunfonaloo is writing a poem
similar to this one.
She is saying that she will also reach for the stars
and write about someone named me writing this poem.
Sunfonaloo, how are you doing today.
Sunfonaloo: In our culture we don't interupt people
when they are writing poems.
Well I apologize, Sunny, next time I'll send a missile.
Sunny's people are now preparing to attack planet earth.
But we will be gone by then,
already migrated to a certain planet in Galaxy 657,
and we will have changed our names to things like
Sunfonaloo. Sunfonaloo, how did your poem turn out?
Sunfonaloo: Well I just copied one I wrote on earth
a long time ago when I lived there.
It was a poem about reaching for the stars.
Oh how nice, Sunny, it seems that you copied me.
That is why we plotted to destroy your planet
and you guys defended yourselves by attacking us
so we migrated to your galaxy and then
it turns out that it was us all along.
Who are you going to blame now Sunny.
Sunny you should try not to bother anyone next time
and just write a nice little poem like this.

Poem

what if you went to
A mock Christmas party
Where everyone ate cookies and punch
Sarcastically

Poem

Stores should make video cameras
that are also guns

Poem

What if you named your pet guinea pig
"grandmother"

Poem

Philosophy club
What if God is playing God.

bad mothers

When life is
Like an obstacle course
Slightly misaligned
So you always get the opposite of what you work for

Ten o'clock chicken stock

If I ever work in a hospital
I am going to fall down every day for attention

Above all else

Our hearts are lands under seige.
Whose side will we take
When someone is in torment,
Or just bad.

Would we not want to be a battle hero
Shielding someone
From an army of spears?

To Spare a spear
Spear the spares
Spur the spire.

the gospel

God died
And we found out
We are included in his will

**the aggressive community
Of intellectual challenge**

It actually is both things.
I have to play stupid to talk to you
And I genuinely don't understand
Because you're an idiot

my Indian name:

Not thankful enough for vegetables

If you don't know what this means

pen name: sour grapes

diagnosis: racism

It's an interesting narrative that almost makes as much sense as any one of my hundred stories that tell the truth instead.

No one is saying the thing I am keeping to myself except maybe it is a key factor in my own vision and acceptance of the persecution.

To turn in my overlapping economies, a dearest discovery exchanged for one world where it's all cash, all blessings, and the most outrageous insult, the intolerable injustice of a third lost chunk of transcendent life and ultimate contribution is really unmerely the most exquisite gun metal dice set available to a post corruption immortal like myself, and an indestructible treasure that can and will be rolled to allow for an extra turn in heaven's game with a route through the mountains of corporation freedom joke world fifty five. What does this mean. What am I talking about. You don't spend your life working for the benefit of the people just to have some weasel swindle the world with a false paycheck or a whip or video, or a bathroom monitor reminiscent of the wrong song dead fire zapper.

When no weapon formed means all weapons formed, then someone has a problem, and I wont be a fool to assume no dice, no lice, thanks gice.

diet for the new continuum

taking a turn for the radical
doing some work for sabbatical

this is a rhyme that chose to stay
and be a part of quite a day

when all my innards cramped within
to say they know where food has been.

but i am doing fine right now
and ate some beans and rice and cow.

next time be more calm and nice.
and drink some water with your ice.

poem

you dont have to concede, you dont have to secede.
you dont have to exceed, you dont have to expel or repel.
you can just be a presbyterian.
it sounds complicated but that is so it will be a surprise
when you find out you dont have to do anything.
like not even clean your apartment
do dishes
care about anyone
or stop the inappropriate fixation on mice and rodents
which might have been the secret all along anyway.

God is saying to everyone
I told you not to squawk wrong
or say you don't want a birthday present on halloween.
I will think of something to say, too,
like how am i and how are you.
now i say the code once more
thats 5168234.
it unlocks a building near
down the street on second pier.
there are treasures, food and ham
unless i'm joking which I am.

Jeopardy Faggot Crap

blue nazis raping christian teens.
that is what everyone is paying for.
green slime from the new york times
delivered to your doorstep.
you share an ad on facebook
but they change it to something else
when it posts,
just to show who's in charge:
the noids from dominoes pizza.
i knew when i saw them on tv as a kid
and that is why i added some parables to the bible.
the one about winning plinko
on price is right,
spinning the wheel,
one dollar,
the showcase showdown.
winning it all
as long as you promise not to hell.

What makes a home a home

A home is a home when the rooms are not clean,
When walls have some dents and the window's unseen,
The carpet has splatters and tables are filled
When messes are everywhere-- stuff is all spilled.
I'll say what I'll say without being constricted,
A home's most a home once we all get evicted.

My apartment

Moldy soup, mice, half eaten candy on the floor,
If I write a poem about my apartment,
It kind of sounds like the legal documentation
That my landlord has probably been listing
To try to get me kicked out
So the company can raise the rent on the next person.
Well then I will let them write the poem for me
And they can turn it in to a poetry contest on judgment day
Where the prize is to have a landlord like themself.

A memory of home

There used to be a scary story where
Someone put a puzzle together
and it was a photo of the room they were in
And as they finished the puzzle,
there was a mad man standing behind them.
Well I had a similar experience
Except it was a cartoon puzzle with
Some cute little quails in the corner.

Poem

If I was the fbi
I would disguise myself as
a marching band
in a parade.
I think no one
Would ever suspect that.

Pandemic

A crisis,
Or relief
for a worse crisis?
Finally the sky is falling.
God is going to save us.

"We're all the worst people we have ever known."

Ok, sure, that's fine,
but honestly
some people have been
really nice to me.

Theology Treatise

What if the meaning of life
Turns out to have something to do
With one random guy
Eating a piece of pie in Kansas.

Well we know that is not true
Because of the Bible.
But we don't know what is true
Because we haven't read the Bible.

Speak for yourself.
Okay.

Whitey and the man are mad at me.

It is because I said I was Jesus Christ.
But really I am not.
But they are mad because
I ate a museum for lunch
Except it was a sandwich.
There will be a court case now
But people have to think of their arguments
Based on a combination
Of scattergories and boggle.
What is red and white and blue
And ruined all over by the newspaper--

Museum writing

This poem reminds me of the time I went to a museum
Because of the way this poem
Refers to that time that I went to the museum.
That is what I meant when I said
"This poem reminds me of the time I went to a museum."
It is a literary reference to this poem
About the time I went to a museum
And the time I wrote about going to the museum
And the time I referred to writing this poem about
Referring to going to the museum.
Another interesting thing about it
Is that I could be at a museum right now if my apartment
Got moved to a museum exhibit without me knowing it.

Comedy Routine in Progress

You know how they have Chinese New Year?
Well what if they had Chinese Groundhog's Day.
Instead of seeing his shadow it would be like
Does the groundhog get eaten or not?
That does not seem right.
But I am from South Carolina
where honestly there is some racism.
In the North they say
What is your preferred pronoun?
In the south we say
what is your preferred slur?

Place Prompt

The prompt for the writing group was to write about a place that no one knows about but you. I had trouble thinking of something but thought it could be funny if I ended up sharing my writing in front of everyone and told people that the place I chose was Satan's lair.

It is an empty dark place and I can only see a small area and stn in goat person form is standing there waiting for Allison.

It is her fault but I do not wish for her to have to be bothered every day forever by a bad thing.

So I decided to try for the forgiveness and when the youtube song sounded like her I was like maybe it worked.

Then today I imagined myself sawing stn in half and I was able to because he was lifeless and frozen in a certain way. So I just sawed him in half and it was not gorey.

So I would think that it would solve the problem but Allison could still end up getting in trouble for a long time but I think that it is more likely that she will be my nemesis in purgatory for several million years like gamers.

What about marion. I don't know.

Interestingly the place associated with him is the music department. So maybe that was nice of him. He used to have a houseboat. Well that is from the conspiracy probably because when I was a kid I thought houseboats were cool. People are saying it has to do with a pontoon boat. Those kind of boats are not cool. Speedboats are not cool either. Rowboats are cool.

Rafts are okay but rowboats are the right kind of boat for people on a lake.

What have we learned. Rowboat picnics, possible fishing but probably not. Probably feeding ducks. But ducks are not on that kind of lake. But maybe some ducks are on that kind of lake.

Really that is not usually the kind of lake. That means trespassing is necessary.

I do not think I really sawed stn in half. But I thought what if for my purpsoes I did like that was the endgame.

Well we know it is not because of marion who is still on the loose.It seems that this was predicted by the people who tried to get me to paint a Haitian revolutionary on an elementary school wall. Well it turns out he was a nice guy but Wikipedia said he attacked the French settlers.

Well to me then that means you have to question George Washington. Which I always questioned. I knew we were wasting our time with those guys. Paul revere was not that bad but not as good as the people who work at the grocery store and advertise for paper towels.

This has to do with philosophy but it might be the excuse prepared for the excpected problems. Well that would reverse the something.

I am sitting in my chair. It is fun but I saw a good chair on the sidewalk the other day and it reminded me that there exist in the world small cushioned chairs like recliners but shorter and closer to the ground. Well I like that kind of chair. Well maybe I could order one to be delivered to my apartment. But my apartment is very messy and maybe this chair is fine.'

Well maybe this chair is tired of being harassed and appearing on zoom.

Maybe the other chair in my aparmtnet could be switched with this chair and then I could sit in that chair.

Why did the conference people not use my pen name on the schedule. Sometimes it seems okay. sometimes I feel mad.

They are saying don't be jealous and cave in to people's legal onslaughts. Okay.

That is not what I am saying. I am saying the people are saying you think you stole the recipes but you did not and started believing that you did. But you wrote it ten years ago. And you should not have to tear up your book because of the people who try to hurt the people every day. I am going to say some crazy stuff everyone but I will try not to hurt people.

Thank you for calling CVS pharmacy

I personally
Don't think God was being sarcastic
On the cross
Or in the Bible.
People laugh sometimes
Like when they are kids
And someone doesn't give them some candy
And they act as if it is
A crucifixion of sorts.
Which it kind of is
If it has to do with Glenn and the strawberry candy.
Glenn, I don't think I took advantage
And it's not your fault that I did not
Get to be a science puppeteer.
Anyway, only 5 cents
For something very yummy
Unless it is medicine for 25 dollars
Plus your wasted life keeping insurance.
They are saying you don't care about the mice in your apartment,
But why else the crumbs.
Why else the court case on the drug store phone
which is being recorded for Judgement Day.
It will be so weird when the real Supreme Court
Turns out to be in a meadow somewhere
Near some trees,
Or at a restaurant where the good people
Always order oatmeal out of politeness.
A litmus test based on either
Random manners on a Saturday
Or the perpetual state of a human heart,
Destined to be found out as either
A fabric and liquid machine spewing acidic hatred
Or a galaxy too beautiful to behold
except over some span of eternity.

Should I make this poem an epic poem,
And say that if you read it, you have to eat it,
In either paper format or shards of computer glass?
Otherwise you will be on the list for the curse of earthloss,
which is a real curse, you know, from an apple tree
That some people say they don't believe in.
I don't believe in apples, either,
Except at Christmas when people scatter the popcorn.
That is a reference to the great rhyme of game war junction,
Near the bad people's monitoring system,
Where they watch the video tapes
Of grocery store transactions.
This poem was over a long time ago.
See if you can find the real last line.
You can't, can you? Because the poem
Made you remember
That you have a bag of strawberry candy in the
Kitchen drawer labeled consortionism.
I have used that idea before, haven't I?
Well people told me to recycle
Right when I most needed a plastic bag.
Except you think that might not be when I most needed the bag,
But that the other times were times
When I did have a plastic bag, so I did not notice.
Well that is why we should all be punished for everything we do.
They should call jobs "punishments,"
And when people turn 18,
They should go to school to help them decide
Where to go to be punished.
People are mad at me now and say life is already like that,
Except some people think school is like that
And not work, which is why the stupider people
Get paid for knowing about phones and subtraction,
but if you think a thought while staring out a window,
Your mom will find out and you can't ever own a house.
It is from one of the other rule systems,

Enforced by secret shoppers that are traded among companies.
So we don't really know who is who
When we are in our neighborhood.
The pharmacy people
Could be the cops
Who are following you
Because of the report from that guy
Who hummed the wrong way on the bench.
Well he is not necessarily from the political network,
Except by coincidentally being as offensive,
And having a name that they can't spell,
Because they only know how to tear up things
Instead of calling someone with good news.
So here we are again,
Back to the whole main idea
That was challenged in the beginning,
Which was caramel sauce on fried bananas.

A time travel story

Ralph Ralpherson decided to time travel to the future. He chose a day ten years from then and transported to a location. When he arrived, he saw that there were one hundred Ralph Ralphersons already there because he decided to time-travel to that same destination a hundred times again after discovering that he would eventually do that.

This is Art

many blood types for a crimson stain
but only wrinkles in the brain.

i'm going to take all of jesus christ's money
and I am going to buy everyone's soul
and then force them
to each eat a piece of my
exploding full intestines
until all that is left of me
is a glowing rainbow wisp
that has one word left in life
and chooses to say
"you're a faggot, Mikey."

Commentary:

Do you guys think I should have included that poem?
I sometimes struggle socially.

Dear self,

I would try to do the best you can if I were you because certain stuff is going to bother you when the conspiracy reminds you and everyone else of every single mistake you have ever made and then everything gets used against you in a court case and certain details become representative of you and chronically associated with you as an author and written in the bio of kids text books that you did such and such and such and such and you admitted to thoughts of such and such under oath and then there is video that goes viral on twitter and then it becomes part of history like sylvia plath put her head in the oven it will say they showed this video of refried bean who did such and such and ate some chocolate chips at work which is a fireable offense and then the photo of you shooting a bird at that old white man and then a cell phone recording of you calling people names in your neighborhood and then it gets put as a soundbyte in a e-textbook for middle schoolers. Well I guess maybe they will all get a kick out of it like me and todd and them used to laugh in tenth grade about sylvia plath and the iron lung. That is fine I guess I should do some more stuff on purpose.

Create a utopia:

My utopia would be in a tall building that seemed corporate and there would be a cafeteria and then on the next floor is a huge complex with a lot of ratty couches and poofy chairs and some refrigerators and tables and a lot of games. And there would be a section with windows and a section with bookshelves. And people could have computers and do zoom calls. Life I guess is pretty good the way it is but this is also a good utopia to have some tall buildings. And then the elevator could go to the basement which has mazes of candy aisles and an underground river that goes to other lands where there are orchards with lakes and fishing boats and fruit trees with buildings that have concessions like cider and donuts etc and then the mountains are in the distance and a bus takes people to the mountains through some fields where you can feed cows and other animals bagels. Then the bus flies back to the tall building and drops people off on the roof landing and then everyone takes the elevator back to the couch place and then there is a conference room and people do some creative projects that get distributed to a lot of other people who are very entertained. Then people sleep on the couches and order some pizzas and Mexican corn, bacon tomato and goat cheese sandwiches, chicken, hot chocolate, cream sauce, biscuits, caramel, and some other party food. Then everyone wakes up and gets feedback about the creative projects and works on some other funny stuff and makes some comedy videos that are very funny and then they get in trouble but on TV they watch the cops go to the wrong building and arrest some other people.

**Happy Groundhog's Day, everyone.
Here are some valentines I thought would have gone good
together:**

Judgement Day Case Management

i can kind of see what happened and believe some of the stuff i
could not believe for a while about people actually hurting me on
purpose. I basically applied for the job at barnes and noble still
hoping to work in advertising. My resume was amazing for a
beginner advertiser but there arent really entry level jobs for
someone like me without going to do more school which I knew was
not really going to happen. But I still thought I could find an ad job
but I forgot to look for junior copywriter jobs and did not do a good
job search. Meanwhile the medicine I was put on to prevent manic
episodes was absolute chemical torture on the level of being
kidnapped by ISIS. So I felt too hopeless to keep searching for a job
and continued working at barnes and noble in excrutiating agony
with a controlling mom and family problems also adding to the
absolute horror. Then in my mind daydreaming helps and I become
addicted but of course keep doing well at work. But I am wearing
jumpers and skirts because of my gender insecurity and my feeling
like I am supposed to dress up instead of wearing what I would want
to wear which is cool casual clothes. So Barnes and Noble thinks I
look too much like a Bob Jones person when they already have a
Bob Jones person, and they also start to suspect an evangelical ploy
where I am a pawn planted there and not really in it for the cash.
They said that on multiple occasions when I picked up my check
later than normal. But it was a check for 160 dollars for full time
work, so all I could do was save it anyway because I could not move
out of my parents house where my mom is responding to my
tortured state by trying to control and console in a way that is worse
than the torturesome medicine and worse than the work experience
which becomes increasingly worse with weirdly mean customers
and people stealing cds to run out the back door so I have to monitor
something I have no control over. Then the company figures out I
have maladaptive daydreaming and dissociation so they send their
social workers in to try to document any utterances that they can use
as blackmail against me if they get caught doing their other tactics to
make me quit. Then I get on their insurance and it is a life or death

situation where if I curse at anyone in my mental illness tragedy
then I can never be insured for manic depression ever again. And
the medicine costs probably about 400 dollars a month, which is
what, three fourths of my salary. And I start getting therapy which
was helpful but I could not go that often because of my schedule.
Really I needed a medical leave of absence but no one offered it and
instead I was made to feel like I could not take a vacation or the
store would explode. That was an effect of the increased stress and I
believe I did miss my vacation week that year which could not be
cashed out according to company policy because they are greedy
and bad to the core and always have been. But they were happy to
let me lose my vacation because it supported their case that I didn't
really need to be there for money and I was an evangelical plant.
They might have thought that because Young Life was on my
resume even though I had quit after becoming worn out with them in
a similar way. Like I didn't match their branding so they steered my
experience towards quitting. But it wasn't so much a style or
nerdiness problem as much as a gender problem which they sensed
but I did not realize. However I was already suffering from an
erosion of social status because of it, and at Barnes and Noble, they
prided themselves in gay rights activism and felt that my jumpered
self was a threat to that. And I did express objection to their ACLU
shelf display once because it seemed like it was marketing that
represented us in a certain way and I was young and did not realize
what kind of powerlessness I was really dealing with in a store with
the mix of merchandise they had, which they start conspicuously
having secret shoppers buy and focus on in provocative ways to try
to trigger me to quit. But I eventually am trapped there to keep
insurance and the heartbreak of it all just makes my dissociation
worse. But it happens that I had just recently been in the newspaper
for being missing and going to Bellevue, and it was a miracle so
some church people pay attention to my crisis and know also from
my young life days that I have severe family problems. Basically
my mom has autism like I do and my mom thought no one would
know if she controlled me to be trapped and not move to Atlanta
where I could have more opportunities and where she suspected I

would be gay. But at the time I still didnt know that is what it is all about. Well Barnes and Noble and their social workers figure this out and justify in their minds their growing obsession with me because some nice church people actually come into the store to check on me sometimes. It could not have been more minimal and it saved my life. They wanted my daydream problem to seem like an inappropriate fixation on customers but it simply wasnt and was actually well rounded with content with a focus on characters winning awards, and then I buy CDs to feed it. Which they think is more evidence they can use against me if anyone ever questions why they would fire me if they decide to, or if they get in trouble for doing their constructive dismissal, which they have probably done to thousands of employees over the years. Meanwhile, bad insurance policy continues with discrimination against people with pre-existing conditions. Barnes and Noble uses this to keep employees without paying them good wages, and they decide to never adjust my wage to a better wage from what I started with as I become a full time lead bookseller and slowly adapt to the misery of staying there for twelve years. Church people keep being nice to me and try to rehabilitate me and friends create a conspiracy of attention for me that grows more elaborate over time and helps me endure as I replace the daydreaming with a prayer habit that is constant and creative. Barnes and Noble on purpose keeps me scheduled at roles I am weak at, like alphabetizing, so that I wont be too good at my job and make them powerless to fire me, which they already feel like because I tell the truth every time despite their main tactic of pressuring people into lying when we cant find books. But they make the books out of place on purpose and send mad people to ask us for stuff we dont have but i had the courage to say, "The computer says it is here but I can't find it." I do this with intense fear and shame hundreds of times, never with a motivating feeling of success, and a constant fear of losing insurance. So eventually their treatment of me has become criminal and they might know it or might really be used to this because it is their business model of constructive dismissal. The conspiracy of friends around me becomes more supportive in the community as I start writing poetry,

being in a writers group, and eventually going to converse college to
learn how to be an English teacher after reading so many books to
try to be a good bookseller. Still there is no sign of compensation
for my college degree, and this is probably related to them feeling
aware that there has been community organizing and it could be
religious in nature. They monitor my relationship interests because
it seems so relevant if I am decidedly not being gay, but it could hurt
their case against me if i am gay. So people torture me relationally
which is possible because of my schizoaffective disorder that makes
me think people like me when they might not, and causes me to
interpret extra secret messages in addition to the conspiracy's
entertainment and care. But I still mostly identify as manic
depressive as part of an effort to be as strong as I can and postpone
indulging in the benefits of being mentally ill, which include
receiving comforting care. But my crisis is too extreme to receive
that kind of intense treatment, and whenever I have a manic episode,
I can see a risk from the hospital of them not realizing how
dependent I am on insurance and keeping my job.

Then I start a long distance poetry program and those people
know something is wrong and help me recover, possibly reporting
things to authorities as well. Barnes and Noble freaks out after
already tracking me all along and oddly a barnes and noble manager
from another store was in a class of mine at converse and got mad
when some students pointed it out. It was a class that had to do with
lit crit theory and includes racial topics. Barnes and Noble then
increases their attempts to bring out the worst in me and make me
seem like an out of control lunatic who depends on the store for
mental health but offers nothing in return. The conspiracy knows
this and copies what they have observed for ten years. meanwhile
there are now probably experts on the case from my school people
and barnes and noble knows it and decides to do anything to try to
take me down, especially with embarrasing material and all the
deliberate increased stress, especially when I am cashiering in the
cafe, because that is where so many people can be witnesses. And
they can harness the snobbery and discrimination against me for my

continuing gender problem and then make it seem like I am just not a quality nicely groomed employee, meanwhile also continuing to use my youth and demographic as porn food for customers who keep an eye on all the employees as they use porn in the store. So this way I can have the worse of both worlds, except it isnt just two things, it is 30,000 abusive customers each with their own unique attack. This allows Barnes and Noble to send bad people in who are already camoflauged and they can do anything just to rush things along and increase the pressure so I sound impatient and look ugly in front of my community. The idea is to disincentivize the supposed politically motivated evangelical coup which they thought was the problem in the first place because my resume was so good and then I stayed there for 7 dollars an hour. but really they have changed goals and it is less about getting rid of me and more about ruining me in front of everyone and possibly in front of christian history as a poet which to them is the thing that could make up for their embarrassment of me turning out to be a good writer after all instead of just the ignorant southern racist that they wanted to chariactature our whole town as. and if any of them really did feel like there was a ministry happening in an unauthorized way, they would have to ignore a lot of the reality that should have been totally apparent early on, which was that my life really was in crisis and in danger from mental illness and I did have to sincerely stay at Barnes and Noble and was a well read good bookseller who always did better than they deserved.

Well at poetry school it is a miracle and I write a thousand poems and a hundred stories, and now they have a problem on their hands and know it. But I dont know it, so I dont understand when the abuse escalates to the point where I am full of rage and having seizures and cursing under by breath. At some point Barnes and Noble just decides to make that as bad as possible and they think that their predatory managment harrassment and abuse can simply be viewed as not offering the extravagant accommodations that I never requested anyway. So the store manager talks to me only in legal threats and I am now in legitimate ethical dilemmas because I

have no one to report abuse to. But I finish my MFA program and
then apply to NYU social work school, which is immediately on to
Barnes and Noble's little games. Barnes and Noble knows this so
they continue to follow me in New York City and try to document
any behavior they can try to use to hurt my reputation. Their best
bets are racism and child abuse, which someone with disorganized
schizophrenia and now intrusive thoughts from their sexual abuse
can look very guilty of in public or in a court situation. A jury could
be easy to fool, and a rabid crowd looking to hunt racists. So the
NYU people help me survive, along with my creative writing school
people, and probably some cops and FBI people, and Barnes and
Noble will want to say I received unfair favor from hospitals and
schools and affiliates of their company people. But really it is a
torture case that went on for a full twelve years and then
outrageously eight more years after I finished working there. And I
have to watch Twitter explode with everyone else's literature after
writing kind humor as a severely depressed lonely persecuted
schizophrenic who did not have medical care for the disease that
was keeping me trapped on insurance and trapped in a place with
mental abuse that was underestimated because people think that
stuff doesn't count. They think I dont count, they think the abuse
doesnt count, and they think they can do anything they want
anyway, so their crimes dont count because they are the political
anti-religion heroes who secretly kind of wanted Barnes and Noble
to count as a humanist church anyway. Meanwhile, by now, the
conspiracy includes hundreds of thousands of people and there are
probably thousands of legal sharks for barnes and noble who
decided somewhere along the way that it was mutual and a war and
just on too big of a scale that they dont have to factor me in as an
individual. And the people like Allison and Marion as managers
who made their choice to maximize the embarrassing music and
humiliating pornography atmosphere and increase stress and
decrease hours etc, think that really because of the conspiracy, they
are torture victims too. Except that no one hurt them at all except by
being nice to me and helping me stay alive. And they will say that it
was all a defamation campaign all along and that was why they sent

people in to hurt me when I was severely depressed and dissociating. And they feel like they could say anything in court anyway because I had a million conversations in that store and people could believe I said anything. And they think they have me documented as a racist probably based on membership card sales or something, when meanwhile, a membership program at all is as much in a direction of favoring some customers and witholding benefits from others, that it is already by nature probably the more racist thing. But that could be just a decoy for the fact that what they really want is to have their own doctors examine my condition for the trial so they can say it is not trauma. What a fun exam that could be, because we need to rule out cancer on any part of the body and I am bashful from autism and really will refuse to be examined. So the NYU people try to be reliable but seem like they could be biased because my poetry could really help them as a school, couldn't it. But not if I say certain curse words that get me canceled on social media. So it works out well for barnes and noble that i have corpolalia as part of my trauma symptoms which is essentially uncontrolled cursing like torette's syndrome. Kind of a sad plight for an evangelical, but all was already lost in a career selling witchcraft books and pornography, though that might have been mostly minimal and it just seemed like the main detoured purpose of my life because Barnes and Noble sent customers in to buy that stuff as a power play which turns out not to only be individual but directed at whole communities. But they arent the only ones doing that stuff and now have only the hope that their mass abuse will blend with the culture and country's crisis and deterioration and strife. but meanwhile, it has become such a violation that it can only probably be settled on judgment day. But little did people know, that I was so panicked and devastated to know my whole life was being ruined just in those first two years, that I asked God to cash out my whole reward in heaven ahead of time. So some of judgement day could happen early. But we do not know. I do not think it is too late for anyone to go to heaven. But it is too late probably for any jail sentence to be enough for any of the main bad people. what about their secret shoppers and social work people.

Well we might not know who those people are except if they want to try to make me look bad in a trial. kind of funny too that the racial appropriation turns it all into just a game of trying not to say the n word. Like that's all there is left is to not say that word. try not to call allison the n word or anything else like contempt of court.

gice i just dont think i can change any of it except i think
something left out is their basis for the child abuse accusations
which has to do with my immaturity and liking muppets. that will
have to i think be its own subject matter for a different time. very
early on i sometimes felt the possibility of being accused of that.
 probably triggered on purpose by social worker customers and then
they watch me consider it in my mind. but every time i thought it
was ludicrous and always based pretty much on me looking at book
illustrations of googly eyed creatures and liking those books. and
that was literally all there was. and then when i try to put the frog
stuffed animal on my register or i like the black elf dolls everyone is
looking at me like something is wrong. like all the customers are not
laughing along.

but i have simply abused no one. regular stupidity or
awkwardness sometimes, and some bad judgment, but nothing
criminal. though it was quite a risk in those conditions to go teach
high school. but i did fine. a few weird problems like on that test
but mostly nothing truly bad. basically once again everyone got
more than their money's worth.

anyway i think that is that. it seems that covid is a problem
right now. to me there is some major media failure to care about
some places and not others unless they can use it for their political
narrative while people die. instead of helping with outreach from
places that got hit first and knew what to do. but anyway i kind of
want to take a walk but sometimes it is not worth it.

i think in a way i dont have to crack the code on the muppet
thing and i can just sit back and let them crap themselves if they
really think they have a case based on anything.

ok i am adding this later too which is that one of their strategies
might be to try to get the word "pedophile" into the mix of case info
even if it is from establishing that i have that kind of OCD or any
OCD at all. That kind of OCD actually is common and happens to

good people but wasn't a part of my problem during most of the years there. But they probably think both the jury and the public will be pretty stupid and now I have all kinds of instrusive thoughts to be hurt with as they probably try to bring kids to put near me at the coffee shop I go to and then want to subpoena the video of me looking insecure and even scared because of the torment that they themselves caused by attacking all of my social interaction and mental health. what a bunch of losers. and they think if they establish that then they have magically proven that all of the people who have ever been nice to me in any way were basically accomplices to child abuse. And really that is also one of their ways of trying to make it all seem mutual and accuse anyone who helps me survive as also being torturers or accomplices. Meanwhile I can't go to support groups in peace because Kesner interupts me on purpose to try to make me seem mad at him in a bad way. And Jack and Jordan also obviously wanted to be called a name but I continue with my policy of acceptance at school and support group, too sacred to be ruined. They will call that grace a cheap ploy to try to keep their supposed evidence collected by following
me inadmissible in court, which probably would be right if it was a good court. But that could help them too because it would prevent their sharks from being busted through the "discovery" process where other crimes come to light. And that is just for one of the trials that is lined up. Who knows how many they would try to interupt my life with. There could be quite a line of people who think they can cash in if I become successful. Another back up strategy is probably to wait until I make money with books and then to take it all through defamation accusations so ahead of time they try to make everything seem about them or even have to be about them by ruining my life so thoroughly and then later demanding my money and anything else i have by saying it is all a lie. All of it seems to hinge on them being found not guilty for torture, which they assume is likely because it took thousands of people to destroy me and that is just too many people sharing the blame. That is why they thought they could get away with it and why most people think that no one will ever be held accountable for how workers are

treated in stores and restaurants and everywhere. Which again comes back to the interesting topic of wages, still suspiciously low for people now risking their lives all over the country and world.

I think the final issue has to do with reporting abuse of any kind and whether there are bad people or even good people who figure out that they were truly damaged by any of the outrageous problems at Barnes and Noble or during any other time throughout the conspiracy and my survival with mental illness. And that is where I think they want to say that by staying alive and benefiting from any of the attention, then I continually agreed and updated agreements to a social contract supporting all behaviors of anyone in the conspiracy or work environment. Well that is rather ludicrous, like for someone to not commit suicide means that they have signed off on all the world's wrongs and problems as if they are okay with all of reality. Some Presbyterians do kind of view all history as God's plan, and mindfulness people are especially bad about choosing "radical acceptance." However, I mostly take a more Catholic approach with my life participation and do not appreciate or agree with injustice for anyone.

People seem to have gone after my potential and all my careers even before they happened, including my social work aspirations which now have a license behind them. Will people try to take that away, too? I do not know. I think some would want to say that if a child or legitimate abuse victim becomes part of the means to take away my license, then the shame of that would be another crime against them caused by people who support me in any way. Well that is where it gets a little weird, and people might have to be reasonable and take things on good faith and at face value. And the simple fact is that it took me years to become a social worker and it is probably not my destiny to be a child abuser in any way.

So what did Allison really do to me directly through management? It would have to be pretty bad or obvious to be proven as torture. There were a lot of things happening in the store, and about twenty direct management actions that I concluded were part of something called a constructive dismissal, which is a classic form of workplace abuse. It has to do with making work conditions intolerable on purpose. But people don't usually die from it, which I probably will in about 7-8 years. So the question is why did Allison do something so bad and why are people still so confident that they will get away with it? Well I am wondering if Allison figured out that it was a torture case many years before I did, so she tried to establish a defense all along by making me seem bad in various ways, letting things get kind of loose and easy at the store, and then abruptly changing conditions so it would literally snap my neck. Like all of a sudden there are risks of going to jail, losing more than insurance, having my life's work in poetry not be worth it, or what actually did happen which is severe disability with brain injury that will eventually cause all my organs to fail and already keeps me from socializing in ways that are more rewarding than full of loss. So she and Marion and maybe a few other bad Barnes and Noble people figure out that in fact they could be facing torture charges, which they are going to say are false but put them in danger from the whole town and conspiracy that was so clearly supporting me as a bookseller and writer. And on that basis, they will say they could at the time do anything to me and it would be self defense. So they have to create a scenario at least in people's minds that they are the victims or at least threatened by possible attacks from almost anyone. And they will say that if they were faced with the possibility of someone being mad on my behalf and coming in the store at any time to "defend" me, then their tactics are actually a form of peaceful protest compared to what they could have done which was murder me right then. Like all they did was schedule me with people who were also struggling, remove the register codes so that anyone could be blamed for theft, which hey, doesn't that benefit me, too, and then just capture everything on video so people can review it later. Well that is just really clever and maybe hard to fight against except for the fact that I was still an innocent person just trying to keep my job and knew that the store managers were hurting me on purpose for no reason and now I am going to die.

Also, I think that at this point, people should not deny that the conspiracy actually worked in their favor, because everyone knew that I had a poetry contribution I was staying alive for, so they let

Barnes and Noble do their crimes to all of us and witnessed it all somewhat helplessly as my life and health were destroyed, along with priceless things like friendships, community service, and future potential to help people with the similar conditions that I already had overcome. That is such a tragedy and as I write this I am surprised myself to think that they would even consider trying to seem like they were the ones in danger. It almost is an admission of guilt itself, like they know that they deserve something bad to happen to them. And they are daring anyone to put a bullet in their brain or preferably in the brain of any of my friends or coworkers or fellow workers at any other store which are now their human shields. And they want to say this post is a crime against them, proving that I deserved to be killed in just the way that they have killed me, even though I was being a cashier keeping insurance with no other motives against anyone at all. I can't help but consider their views a little bit and wonder if salvation could still happen for anyone involved, transforming this case in a way that I would not expect, and contributing to the theological romp that life is. And yet it just seems to be more like something straight from hell, very familiar because of how I felt when I first started working there. It may only be understood on Judgement Day, which is probably why people in the bible say to God, "Better is one day in your court than thousands elsewhere." This concludes my perceptions and recollections of the Barnes and Noble situation that seems to be the reason why people continue to starve me of the normal harvest usually yielded from the kind of work I have done for myself and other people. All that is left is to play this video that I think is similar to what could happen in some people's near futures:

see: raiders of the lost ark final scene on youtube

journal

Gice I think when the bad person was giving odd attention to john awad it was meant to communicate stuff like how Allison felt that she had plenty of customers to call me ugly in various ways. but also I think she was predicting her role as having jewelry in her snout as the whr of Babylon etc. so maybe that happens to match the poem or maybe it was predicted. Kind of weird if it was predicted. Definitely she stopped managing very early on and started communicating only in coded legal threats. and I think that is weird enough that you don't necessarily report it if it feels like it is from the corporate level too. You just try to get through it. weird that destroying the literary legacy was such a goal. It does have the opposite effect of endorsement like a satanic attack does for ministry people. so was the whole thing written by Scott turow and David baldacci as a literary legal thriller? I mean maybe so and it is kind of funny to just go ahead and assume that and turn it in to God that way as a movie. it is kind of like a hallway of doors when you think of all the other lives involved and so many people who did what they were supposed to. I think that was part of it all along was always someone doing better in some way which I still support but I don't support wasted food on the scale of my lost writing appreciation. that is not right and I will not pretend it is okay. but since I feel hopeful there is no need to wallow in despair and I can remember prayers of giving up levels of things but I just think that there were terms that I was functioning under as a writer and they have been used against me as a trick and a violation and stealing something valuable from a lot of people. And to say it was always hypothetical is kind of like killing someone and saying the rest of their life was never a guarantee.

Martyr Complex

So I guess God was mad because he had just done the most obvious miracle that any of us had ever experienced which was to help me get to Bellevue hospital during a manic episode and kept me safe and sound right when it could have been otherwise. He was acknowledged in the newspapers but then for some reason in Greenville his work of protection was soon counteracted by a complete attempt by many grownup bad people to smother any further faith and loyalty or hope from me ever again. The worst part was the medicine, which was obviously putting me in unbearable agony from day one. That was an innocent mistake from a bumblefuck methodist doctor named James Page. Honestly I am still not that mad at him even though that is the worst of all of the whole mix of suffering which now includes federal crimes and possibly twelve years of attempted murder from a retail store. So what was the other problem? I think another person perpetually confronted by reality without any surrender was and is still my mom whose obvious impairment from autism was also somewhat innocent but still a threat to my life, which became permanently ruined by her successful but wrong and satanically-influenced determination to prevent me from having a career and a person. You try to find an analogy for something like that, but I am not sure there is one unless it has to do with that CD cover at Barnes and Noble with that girl holding a giant snake around her neck. I think it is one of the Barnes and Noble social workers' assessment tools, and could make it into the torture trial when they present the notes on what they have speculated was my daydream from the disassociation that happened from chemical warfare on my soul. I don't know if they bugged the registers or did eye-tracking or just know the most common maladaptive daydreaming elements, but they seem pretty confident that they can base their decision to try to kill me on whatever they think was in my mind as I did better probably than anyone else in the store for many months, getting paid 7 dollars an hour with a little bit too much knowledge of classical music for them to keep pretending that I was incompetent and unpromotable.

But Jeff the manager did let me be a lead music seller and seemed genuinely touched when I offered to pay back the store the five hundred dollars that Kathleen the store manager stole and blamed him for. I guess no need to relive that whole nightmare time that lasted two years but I just didn't know how loneliness worked and why I would feel so much better for a few minutes every time a manager had to come back to the abandoned music department and collect a cash pickup from the register or authorize a return and because of that also say "hello." It was like mild relief from the pain and similar to the 30 minutes of feeling almost normal when we counted down the cash registers in the back office at night and I had other people to talk to but still had to keep quiet when people would say stuff like "Jesus Christ was a fucking lunatic." I think they were trying to get me to say something cheesy like "he is the great psychiatrist" but I knew better and did pretty well with that stuff as the conspiracy stepped in to help me stay alive. A high schooler named Tracy was nice to me and told me a story about someone being chopped up in the bible. Speaking of Tracy and contact tracing, I think some of my loneliness then can partially be traced back to scientific non-advances that just aren't understood yet involving the brain chemicals that are suppressed by psychiatric medicine meant to make you someone else's problem. My theory is that psychosis happens from the brain feeding itself too much dopamine through false consoling thoughts that contradict an intolerable reality, so the antipsychotic medicines reduce that dopamine to prevent delusions. But that creates a double starvation-the original lack of love, and then the prevented replacement love, plus a cap on what potential social food could have been sought out as an adaptation. So that is how my own mind became an opium factory as I imagined comforting thoughts of a happier life that didn't involve myself at all except when one of my artworks was featured on the dorm wall of a daydream character. Barnes and Noble knows the name of that character and so does the whole conspiracy and they have been reminding me of most of the specific content for many years as part of their torture camoflage for the worse legal sharks who still follow me and threaten me. So I don't know how people figured it out but some of it could be from my parents monitoring me which included hovering near my room and blocking the computer and reading all my emails in a way that still makes me wish I was never born. There is a knife in the kitchen that I will use right now if people don't stop torturing me. Anyway I suspected the parental surveillance sometimes but still can't believe the violation and the fact that it may have continued during later years when I was living at home again and using my computer with their wi-fi. I guess they just visited every web page that I visited, which was consistently innocent but eventually included social media pages of people I had crushes on, and then the fact that on their computer system the internet addresses are all now mixed with the internet porn that my dad used on his news feed and which will make the legal sharks think I can't prove their motive which was to desecrate a religious person who conspicuously did not use pornography from the store or internet or TV, and who saved themself for gay marriage while people forced me to view over 2-3 million offensive and embarrassing images in exchange for reliable insurance. Who knows what access Barnes and Noble has to medical records from their baby-killing insurance company, but one strategy that seems clever is to make their insurance network only include a mental hospital with "behavioral health" in the title so it could seem like manic episodes were my own character problem instead of the severe mental illness that they themselves increased to a level where I really could have been picked up in an ambulance at any time day or night for about four years. I had already learned not to get any help for depression, because my family taught me that I deserved pain and punishment for anything I did that was good after my sister suffered from their parental neglect that they wanted to hide by trying to equalize our lives starting in high school when they helped cause me to fail math and get a C in AP English. Well that was Barnes and Noble's tactic, too, to discourage me from doing well and staying there too long as part of their brand crafting and management of "employee traffic," kind of like store traffic which can be sped up by deliberately bothersome music, but it had more to do with managing our lives for us and deciding who could finish school and who could either be promoted to department manager or just stay alive at all. I think it is a stretch to say that Barnes and Noble is why DJ got AIDS, or TJ died in the car wreck, and yet it is likely that Sheron Westmoreland did get sent to the same section of hell as Arthur Miller and Nabokov. But I guess I am conflating the Judgement Day case with the probably national constructive dismissal case once again, though that mix up might be from God himself, because I do remember where I was standing when I first felt the supernatural observing audience for my horrific daydream. I sensed it above me as if from Barnes and Noble's ceiling in actually what was a different section than where the video camera was that Jesse said was fake. It felt like people from heaven or near there were all watching me during a Judgement Day already happening, and viewing everything in my mind with what still feels like a critical eye, though many earth people since then have stepped in and blocked the viewers with their own generous attention and secret messages. Thank you so much everyone, I think a lot of people are excited to be superstars in front of a supporting crowd, and I guess the people who didn't do so well like when that girl stole a sandwich from the cafe refrigerator or when Allison created a two year long video of herself crapping directly into every single Greenville resident's mouth, can try to settle things with God in the quiet space of their mind or the louder arena of shrieking when they are pushed down a slide of cheese graters into a pool of acid in whatever punishment location is worse than hell. It's kind of odd to think of that because it reminds me of the manager named John who used to joke with me about religious humor and literature and I told him that I thought the road to hell was paved with shark skin, which is smooth one way and sharp the other. He liked my joke, and kindness like that saved my life several million times as the lashes in the other direction accumulated and eventually took their toll of me losing a whole literary career and an advertising career and a lost teaching career too after Barnes and Noble exhausted me on purpose at the cash register during Christmas break so I had to grade my research papers at the mental hospital. The hospital knew what was going on more than I did, and now several more hospitals have their

own confirmations to share about the chronic near death experience
that continues every day. I think what they don't realize though is
that now when I occasionally have to call 911 with heart problems,
it still doesn't compare to the life and death nature of each moment
at the customer service desk or behind the register in the cafe during
my life at Barnes and Noble where a parade of customers took turns
trying to provoke me on purpose to lose insurance and my
education. I guess I don't know which customers were their people,
and I used to joke about how funny it would be if there were "secret
employees" like "secret shoppers." Sometimes people laughed at
my jokes; sometimes they didn't. It was kind of weird when that
guy named Matt who also was at the poetry scene I went to at
Coffee Underground and who said he was going to get an MFA too
was assigned to clean up my section that I had to keep organized. I
guess it was to document the difference between my work and his,
which honestly was significant. Kind of funny too that I was
assigned to a section like that which used planograms because
planograms were the reason I decided not to try to be a department
manager and Barnes and Noble knew it. I was certain that
impossible and tedious tasks like that could cause me to lose my job
and consequentially the insurance I needed for a disease that was
way more expensive than my paycheck per month and could
suddenly cost 80 thousand dollars at any time with little to no
warning. But I was used to low job security already because of
Sheron and Howard and Chris and Scott. I think Trevor is innocent,
and possibly the grand hero in addition to Christina, who actually
did let the store know that there would be legal consequences if they
were wrongfully terminated. Trevor made a graph of the quantity of
books the store was receiving and the percentages were much higher
than the stated official ration. So the system was being flooded, but
he stayed strong and kept his paycheck at exactly 40 hours to the
dot. Well I wasn't like that at all, and had a habit of leaving 7
minutes early on most 10-6:30 shifts for some time when Sheron
was the manager, because of the way things seemed to get
psychologically unbearable during that last hour and the store was
eerily quiet with no tasks were left to do. That was when Barndt

was told to write me up on about the second time I was 7 minutes late in the morning right after I moved apartments to a place fifteen minutes away instead of five minutes away. So that was too bad. It just took a while to adjust to the new drive time, and Bardnt was sad that he had to do that to me. There is more that I am not saying because of all the overlapping legal cases that Barnes and Noble probably thought would happen sooner. They just thought I would kill myself every time they played an embarrassing song or sent in a teenager to ask me for a witchcraft book, but I kept staying alive and telling jokes. And I think they thought they could get me to gossip myself into being fired, but I never said anything bad about anyone until I weakly one day answered someone about my preference for manager candidates from the employees who were trying to impress the bad people and earn the new manager spot left by Stephanie in the cafe. I suspect Stephanie of being one of the social workers because of the way she told me right after she started working there that she was going to try to be one of the bosses and I immediately started kind of groveling in a bad way like I always did with the managers who kind of knew it coudn't be helped and that my flattery habit was partially from the feelings of failure the store created on purpose, but also could be framed as part of an annoying personality problem that would justify them going ahead and making it clear that I simply had no real future in the company unless I wanted to be severely clinically depressed for the rest of my life. I think that is why they were so interested in creating scenarios that could establish diagnosis information for the social workers and doctors who were probably from New York and assumed to be more credible than my medical people who I saw only occasionally because of simply not being able to easily schedule or attend an appointment ahead of time with a retail schedule. That was tragic considering that the trap of insurance is what kept me there but I mostly still couldn't get care and relief for severe mental illness. And that was what Sheron was most determined about- making sure I knew I could not use a personal day unless it was scheduled in advance of the two weeks. Like once the schedule was made, I could not use a personal day. Well I know pretty well how the concept of a personal day actually would be more meant for a schedule already made, but that was her clue to anyone looking out for me that she was ready for court at any time. One day, she confronted me at a shelf that I had not alphabetized well, right in front of the gay book section, and she looked at it with me and said, "help me understand what you are doing here," or something like that as she observed that some books were out of order. One time she called us each into the office and said "Are you happy working here?" I think that was so she could say we lied to keep our jobs. That was similar to Allison's methods, too, though Allison would sometimes just look at something and then smile at me as reference to a legal matter, like when I got my new car which I guess they think is a way to hide parental money, or that time when there was a latino therapist doing a booksigning and Allison gleefully "exchanged a glance" with me as if to say they intended to make race part of their legal attack. Like maybe they have something really juicy on me and I just wonder what it is. I think I know what it is which is that they know my daydream characters adopted black kids which I was planning to do but can't because of the psychological problems from the life abuse. But I am fine with it. What I really wanted was for people to know about Jesus Christ. I actually am sad that goal was also thwarted by an eternally damaging ten year delay in publishing after the 2012 tragedy that re-ruined my rebuilt life. Anyway I think that daydream example might not help their case as much as when I described a certain mad customer as "bitter black lady" on my private personal prayer list that I typed one day and years later sent to a seminary with my other prayer grids during a manic episode. I guess the documents made the rounds in our community and found their way to the unitarian people who Barnes and Noble probably worked with and did some collaboration to keep their clientele seeming at least intellectually diverse and to maintain their power over customers who shop in the Christian inspiration section. I think Marcus Borg is acceptable reading to them but that shark who tried to get me to lie about the Stormie Omartian book must want to bring it into the case that I bought a book called "Power of a praying parent." Well I bought that book for myself for prayer ideas, and they seem to think they can turn that whole scenario into a characterization of me using their customers in a weird fixated stalking way to replace an unfulfilled nurturing life dream of some kind while also not being someone they can trust to serve their younger customers who hopefully will get some of the money their parents are paid in order to use them as junior legal sharks. I guess that is why NYU waited so long to confirm the tragedy- so all the kids involved could be older in order to get a more accurate idea of the "damages." I have thought before that maybe their social workers want to say I was "disappointed" in my single status that came from a clear hygiene and grooming problem even though I took a bath every single day right before work, never wore my preferred outfits of overalls and bandanas, and checked in the mirror often throughout the work day to make sure I looked okay and to try to tolerate the challenge of being a stared at as a public figure in the cashiering spotlight of my community every second of my work day despite autism and social anxiety and being perpetually taunted with the obviously preferable but unattainable solution of having the copywriting career I worked 9 years to achieve at any basic level of participation. That actually was a disappointing loss after the medicine and addiction problem, and partially due to unfair insurance laws that enabled people like Barnes and Noble to trap workers like me. Later on I was also in fact disappointed to lose a publishing deal and love interest and school scholarship support because of being suicidal/homicidal towards the old white men who harassed me past any point of tolerance and because of how I was eventually no longer able to read well enough to be an English teacher as planned. Gosh, that goal took about four years to accomplish and then lose, and after that of course the three years for the MFA. So maybe Barnes and Noble was expecting a lawsuit at first but then perceived a more serious potential PR problem which might still be happening based on all the weird phone calls I get and the guy who sat next to me at Staples one day recently in New York City 8 years after leaving Barnes and Noble but who made himself known as a shark when I was writing a blog post there about the Nobel Prize and the guy looked at me in the store in front of video cameras and held out his hands as if daring me to call the cops, which makes me think first of all, that I am being followed pretty closely at all times, and second of all that maybe Barnes and Noble saw something happening before I did and was trying to make me turn out bad in order to prevent their fear of me receiving literary recognition that would embarrass them, or maybe even a suspicion that I was a contender for something more than the literature prize based on my patience with 5 million bothersome things on purpose. Well that is life for most people by now, so I can let that kind of absurdity go, especially since I have such a problem cursing, compulsively making rude gestures, and saying I am going to kill everyone. So I lose even basic Protestant saint status which most people can attain just through faith alone, or by not being gay, yet Barnes and Noble is still worried that I might get any reward whatsoever for good behavior, which is something maybe they did not expect for a while, kind of like me not expecting to live much longer or go to heaven when I die. Anyway I don't know what has to do with what, except that Barnes and Noble might have had people at all my schools and knew also from the private investigators that for most of the time I had not published much as a writer except for a few blog posts like the one where I complained about how teachers always used to lie about the discount program to our face to get 20 percent off personal purchases. It's not a big deal I guess, except that I was making a third of a teacher salary and it seemed kind of disrespectful for people to lie so blatantly, and for me to now know in retrospect that some of it was probably done on purpose by corporate sharks to establish the power dynamic that allowed them to destroy us all.

Anyway that brings me back to the topic of personal days, which is an odd thing to be abused with because I was constantly called in to work shifts for other booksellers who cancelled at the last minute. Like probably up to 200 times without needing that favor myself except for one or two hospitalizations. But that was good people like Mike and April and Kathy who would call me and were counting on me in a good way and I think that could be because Mike knew Sheron was a bad person from having worked with her at Dollar General. Sheron did not like people who seemed to be "privileged," and that is why she made her presence known a time or two when me and Andrea who attended Oxford University used to do guessing games about books. And the up and ups were mad when I used "Madame Defarge" as my cashier name for the membership sales announcements over the intercom. It was supposed to be Disney characters so no one would feel abused or even tortured by someone who they knew was eventually on their way to NYU.

Anyway even though so many people did hurt me on purpose during the last two years there and as a result contributed to a video of me at my ugliest worst self sounding like Gomer Pyle at the over surveillanced cash registers, I think Mike was a good manager who was sending out a call for help and letting everyone know about his certainty of Barnes and Noble's intentions towards me all along and their reasons for ultimately going for the kill. And Kathy stayed neutral as a witness who I remember noticing when that old white guy was rushing me so much in a weird way at customer service. And I think he was targeting her and not me with it even though it hurt me and made me sound impatient as they had triggered thousands of other times. I believe that strategy was to reframe the way I was so fast and efficient about recovering the store and cashiering and customer service: In other words, any part of the job that I was actually allowed to excel at. Jenn G also stayed successful and patient and neutral despite similar impatience from customers and I think it was part of their strategy of making it seem like I should have been able to handle the stress too. I am sure that most of my friends still don't appreciate being used as weapons against my life and all the people in it. Anyway Mike assigned me for 7 hours at the torture register during the last couple of years and I didn't understand the betrayal, especially when he did things like order pens that didn't work to increase the frustration. And then he wrote me up for not putting up the SAT book back on the shelf from the floor fast enough after I had memory problems and eventually dementia at 35 or 36 years old. But now I see that Mike was letting me and others know that some of it must have to do with how I said

"Jesus died for your sins" to customers at the register for several days after that Chinese guy came through the line and then Mrs. Spink who buys SAT books witnessed it and is ready to testfiy, and the SAT book was also an issue because I bought an SAT book once during the original agony years and I was going to use it to create joke tests from an idea I saw in the school brochure of Portfolio Center in Atlanta where I got accepted but didn't have enough parent support to attend. My mom criticized me about that book too and I think it was so I would remember it was on my transaction history which I guess Barnes and Noble sees as relevant to trying to make it seem like I am a child abuser because of my autism which makes me have a younger emotional age in some ways. I guess they have psychology people who will say it is not autism but a personality disorder that annoyed the living daylights out of everyone and would justify their helpless and intensified but still unsuccessful attempts to repulse me from the store. But anyway Mike's actions make me think that he believes it has to do with me being a Young Life leader in college which I have already written about and know that my developmental disorder was not appreciated there either. I guess it is just seen as a risk that warrants making sure I also stay delayed in my spiritual development too and go years without understanding my own religion, only increasing the opportunity for people to trigger my scrupulosity OCD on purpose and convey their opinion of me by saying how much they hate Fox News and Ann Coulter. It took me a long time to figure out they were talking about me because I simply didn't watch any TV at all for most of those years and for quite a while Barnes and Noble was all the socializing in my life.

Anyway I 'm getting tired now and will end by saying I have concluded that schizophrenia is the cure and not the illness. It is what the mind does to adapt to messed up life, and disorganized catatonia and movement symptoms are the most effective organic intervention and should really be seen as a legitimate substitute for medicine instead of a cause for increasing doses. Researchers should see the disease and know that there is a disease behind the disease, and the brain is eating itself to feel better.

I could still at any moment believe that I am the Anti-Christ and just kill myself.

Thank you Patrick, Thank you Llama friend and all the authors and CD DVD people. Thank you Alyssa from Mitchell Road, and thanks Robert for being my friend! Hey Natalie, Hey Valita. Hey Glenda.

Ok I think I can say a little more which has to do with two things: When they got more aggressive with legal threats and witnesses and in-person harrassment, did they supply their own professionals or capitalize on existing networks that overlap with my contacts in some way, and if so, how many of those people were semi-innocent suckers who just made a mistake based on my nerdiness vs how much were those people very savvy hateful ideologues who already were chipping away at christianity or disability or moral standards or whatever else in our town people thought were their enemy? I mean I don't know and maybe that is why the people who delayed the case on my behalf by postponing my literary contribution and work eligibility thought they should let Barnes and Noble be the ones to attack my writing first and show their own people so everyone could see their level of boldness and supposed reasons for their assault on our community. And that is where Barnes and Noble thinks they were justified in feeling like that proves they were up against something legitimate and had to enlist all kinds of bullies more powerful than me. But I think anyone who has supported me also knows that it truly is Barnes and Noble that caused my basic life goals to be thwarted pretty much multiple times over and possibly in totality already, so there is really no instance of legal backing that made those decisions for me. In fact that is probably something my therapist has had to worry about as she makes normal social work case management decisions, or possibly has decided not to at all even in the usual way as a safeguard against being targeted herself.

Anyway I think I could go on about that more but don't know what I am talking about so I will just move on to the next thing which to me is pretty major. And that has to do with what I think their main form of power to really use against employees is and that is their cash register practices when combined with decency laws, especially factoring in things like statutes of limitations. And probably most legal people know that would be their main way of maintaining power over us is to get stuff on their receipt records that they could later say was a crime if we caused trouble. That is where I would say especially at this point that a crime like that has to be seen as theirs alone and any involvement from regular booksellers would automatically turn into an additional crime against us from very evil intentions that to me comprise one of the most compelling reasons to view it as torture based on the absurd proportion between what we were paid in the store and what was at stake in our lives if they succeeded in incriminating us. Like just the threat of it is something to go to war over, which they know and are hiding behind as their explanation for making me seem like a dangerous and vengeful mentally ill person. Which actually I kind of am now but mainly to myself as I imagine violently and suddenly carving an unhealable deadly stab wound into my stomach on the day I find out I have to go to jail for selling the wrong thing to someone. It is my punishment for keeping a job, for finding a way to serve my community, and most of all for staying alive. Blaming Satan isn't good enough for that horror, especially considering all the eager cooperation involved from humans who seem just as bad as any other hellbound thing already and many of which who did find their way to Barnes and Noble for the very purpose of selling offensive material in the Bible belt. That was their goal all along, and as for the risk and responsibility that Barnes and Noble supposedly tolerates heroically for everyone's sake, it was pretty thoroughly heaped on human shield cashiers, including teenagers, and the upper managers who are supposedly in the same boat made a lot more money and had training to know what to do other than just helplessly and hopelessly sell everything with a grief that turns

lifelong within days of working there. And maybe every receipt
ever labeled with anyone's name will eventually be evidence for the
more inclusive Judgement Day case I mentioned earlier. Well that
brings us to the gospel of Jesus Christ which is that heaven is not
that much like Barnes and Noble in some ways and people probably
won't have a list of all their moral failings made public once Jesus is
handling the legal cases in person. And that is the reason people
like me can consider not killing anyone over that cash register threat
I pointed out which I have to say is not a minor detail. Get it?
Minor? like "minors" being sold teen fiction that is more and more
like 50 shades of grey every day but when a fifteen year old buys
that book you only know you are supposed to sell it but have to
worry for the rest of your life if you will go to jail for ten years once
your torturers are arrested. Anyway now that girl will probably be
on video leaked to facebook so the social workers have to factor that
in when they decide who to report what to when. I think they
thought my health was the main priority but I didn't and that was
why I was able to stay alive and work at that stressful place with still
a remnant of purpose in my life. To me this is getting boring now
but I am wondering if for some people the gospel is really "God
hates you." And if that works kind of like the Lutheran theology
which is the idea that when you see that you are a sinner then you
are already almost free, except this concept is more about getting the
rejection from God that you were trying for which ends up being
enough to win you over after all. And that could be why it has felt
so wrong in this culture so often for people to try to share their faith
to unreceptive people when maybe God needed for people to know
that He hates them. Like in an Esau way from the bible which could
still mean salvation. People say that is universalism but to me that is
not automatically the case. And I would probably end with this new
recent philosophical wondering which is: "Are the people in hell
worthy or unworthy of God's disgust?" It's interesting to think about
and if they aren't worthy then wouldn't that mercy turn to water that
extinguishes the fire? Maybe it is both and the experience will
include a variety of millions of years of suffering similar to how
things have already gone on earth. I guess I don't know. The verses

in the Bible that address it are when this guy in hell calls across a chasm that can't be bridged and asks to go warn his father of the torment. But Jesus says no. And it seems like he says no because it is extrinsically impossible like a system that can't be excepted upon but it could be that Jesus says no because he is on to that guy's little games that have not stopped and will never stop and God knows all the intents of everyone so his people who trust him win their lives no matter what the assault is and the bad people lose their lives no matter who wins any legal cases that they made their audacious bad acting performances in. Anyway now all the legal cases have exploded, much like the store should have a long time ago, and thousands and millions of people have gains and losses from all the problems that are very similar to pretty much now everyone's normal life crisis times and sufferings in the country and world. So I hope people have a good lawyer named Jesus Christ or a good judge named Jesus Christ or a good friend named Jesus Christ who will visit them in jail or provide a good church full of Jesus's friends who will come visit you at your job when the New York Mafia starts raping you. That really is all this time and the end except to say that CVS hasn't been that nice to me either and I called the cops about it this week.

Whiteness versus Witness

The black church from a long time ago is probably in heaven now. I do not know how much integration there is with other races in heaven, but probably with millions of years then people can choose to get away from other races like the white people who hurt them or they can live in the same communities and possibly receive some acknowledgement and rewards and repair from the difficult times of slavery and all the oppression after that. But their glory is probably something that people want to be near in heaven too so they might still be patient in some ways.

I do not know if there is purgatory but some people from black churches might be getting opportunities that were denied them on earth but that can only be possible in environments and locations that still have elements of earth's losses. Like if they want to hunt and fight but could not before because of jail and death and abuse, forced labor, stolen wages, or other problems. It is possible that some victims of abortion could be given a chance at life during the millennium in revelation.

On earth the black church is still a witness of God's power and provision of life that can't be destroyed. The churches probably still lack the right amount of tithes because of compounding economic swindles, but they might be doing well in terms of righteousness and praise. But sometimes the bad people try to take away the righteousness, either to prevent it or to take it for themselves later. That could be some of the motivation behind mass incarceration and profit from prisons and police murder, or appropriation and pretending to help.

But this sometimes just increases the witness of the church, causing the bad people's plans to backfire and resulting in more glory and confirmation of God's goodness. The low wages that continue to be a problem for many black people could also add to the hope of better rewards in heaven anyway. It can be a reminder that life on earth is not all there is so don't fall for it and make slavery mistakes.

The black church also continues to have many opportunities for theology and could be able to see some of the bible more clearly than those who are blind in a white way. I have noticed personally that a lot of black people don't assume their survival as much as white people and are often especially thankful for each day of life.

Nation vs Discrimination

This is just a short reflection to say that I like Vernon John's radical sermons and titles for the church signs. I am doing something similar with poetry. I have some extreme lines and blog posts but think in the big picture, my true motivations and love will be apparent and God's mercy, not condemnation. Something I do worry about is that it seems like people who have helped me as a writer think my work might be best for young people, and I hope they can handle all of the controversial ideas. That could have been an issue with Vernon's signs, too, and yet I could imagine kids being able to understand it, especially with extra explanation.

I also really learned a lot from the amazing video and found it to be an interesting picture of religion being applied when some leadership needed to be more civic and derivative. That was just one thought about it. I think my favorite speaker was the guy who spoke about black colleges, which I believe still need a lot more support. There are so many frameworks already and outlets that people could contribute to if they wanted to make a long overdue difference to millions of people still trying to survive and recover from cumulative discrimination, with black churches being some of the best opportunities for support and possibly the most overlooked.

Another thing I am thinking about is one of the questions about the peace mission which has to do with power dynamics. It is kind of scary to think about when focusing on the more cult-like aspects of the group.

And then the last thing on my mind is a growing sense of something I think about a lot, which is the church outside the church. That is a lot of my experience of the church in this life, and I am forming a new concept and awareness of the black church outside the church, like the whole people of God no matter what church participation, and within all of those people, the black portion of all potential and eventual believers, some of whom might not find their way to consistent church membership that is most obvious. I think I have thought of it before but not as much with the frame of really seeing people as the "black church," which I think is a real thing and very useful also for re-examining major concepts of church categories, like branches of Protestantism or Orthodox and Catholic history.

Finally, I will say that as I wait along with everyone else for trump's impeachment and hopefully a successful and safe transfer of power, some of my opposition to trump is not as much of a no-brainer as it is for some people. I think he has been used to portray some Americans and Christianity in a bad way on purpose and I have withheld my full anti-support because of that. I have been up close to a bad side of politics in some of my life and may have an additional obligation to reject racism more publically on the other side as well, which continues to depress me.

Food Ministry Paper

I have three main ideas for actual food programs in New York City, and two ideas for church programs. The three main food ideas are more community based than something to be directly managed by a local church. But a church could take a leadership role in any of the three goals. The population served and serving is likely to include the black church but could also be inclusive in a way that provides an outreach to people of other faiths or who do not have official religious affiliations:

My first idea is a strategy for emergency food distribution during Covid. I shared the idea with some volunteer people earlier this year but think that the city used many other means and locations, and I have not heard of this strategy actually happening. However it is possible that this idea could still be used sometime, and it has to do with having huge trucks of regular food shipments like what would be delivered to grocery stores instead delivered to huge apartment complexes and groups of buildings and then for the food, mostly consisting of multiple servings of a limited number of products, to be distributed either door to door, floor by floor, or to common area locations for residents to pick up in bags. The typical bagging process is actually what I think could be avoided. The image is just of a huge Kraft truck pulling up somewhere in the city, and then volunteers unload boxes of macaroni and cheese and Chef Boyardee and fill the hallways of apartment buildings, knocking on doors and telling people there are some free food supplies. Or canned goods, rice and beans, or juice and milk. To me the Christianity behind it has to do with the resulting sense that food can arrive out of nowhere at any time. I think it would be unexpected in a way that would keep people from automatically becoming too dependent on it too quickly. I think that the reality of it being an emergency provision would be apparent. Different apartment buildings and property companies have different levels of staffing. But if people cared, and even city people when there are no property people to help, then there could be the minimal organization needed to just quickly get food to people. At this point, a lot of food places have created reliable systems with registered recipients, but I think there are millions of people who do not know where to start to sign up for anything and could benefit from a sudden and even haphazard provision like just some brands showing up anywhere that there are a lot of people.

The second idea is similar and that is also an old idea I had and shared unsuccessfully, which is for major candy companies to donate school-wide shipments of candy to locations where the poverty is so extreme that the kids don't ever have any candy at all. This plan is not supported in a lot of places where nutritional deficits are the more urgent problem, but I think that people have underestimated the benefit of a motivating joy like candy in the lives of traumatized children and neighborhoods with a lot of recent immigrants. Some children really are learning by experience that candy is for other people and I think that is wrong.

The third idea is similarly out of sync with many food efforts that emphasize nutrition, and that is an idea for a Junk Food Pantry where there can be a lot of regular clients that are eligible for one grocery bag of treats and snacks per month. It would be managed so that it would not become anyone's steady diet but would be a reliable resource for people who would like to include some kind of comforting dessert or candy product in their lives in addition to whatever they are able to rely on from elsewhere for more normal sustenance. This idea seems now to be not as urgent because of the great need for food on such a scale with many people needing food and resources who are not used to relying on charities and government support. But it is the third idea that I have had in mind as a possible extra link in networks providing for clients who can also benefit from any community involvement and participation. Some food pantry experiences are important socializing opportunities for people. The junk food pantry does not have to serve that purpose but could provide some kind of treat programming as well, or seasonal blessings like report card rewards or book fairs or holiday toy distribution.

I think those three ideas are ideas that I would work on with other people in a context where the basis of generosity could be associated and supported with thoughtful and deliberate church involvement, but with an all inclusive outreach that could also invite other charity-minded organizations to show their participation as well. I actually think a less religious atmosphere would be better so there is no weird feeling and it would be like normal service from people who care, which is likely to include a lot of churches and the larger Black Church within communities.

Another actual ministry that I think can be supported in a good way or replicated in other places are people who take coolers of sandwiches and waters to pass out on the subway. That has been one of the most effective ministries I have seen and I could imagine trying to help with that sometime. The people just get on the subway and ask if anyone wants a sandwich. And some people do need a sandwich. Others donate or take waters.

The last sincere idea I have is for "communion evangelism," using either a truck, like an ice cream truck but with church bells, or just a table in the park or a cart in subways. I think it would require certain gifting and a solid connection to specific churches who take responsibility so that communion is not taken in an "unworthy manner." But one idea behind it is that taking communion regularly while other people don't know to take communion at all could be considered unworthy on some levels. That is just the justification for it but I think if people wanted to offer communion in those disposable cups with wafers in the park and use that as the question to engage people and help them decide if they need more info about God and Jesus or want to just take communion as a believer at an open table, then it could be done well if people were careful. The communion truck is an idea I had a long time ago and that to me could be more like a creative experience, maybe with different options, like there could be a sunday school snack option if someone is not comfortable taking communion or wants to opt for expressing some level of agnosticism then they could eat butter cookies with apple juice. And if people want a free new testament or something they could choose that or maybe a coffee. I think the branding and strategy of all of it would have to be blessed and organic and consistently staffed by confident mission-minded people. And it might be less about the evangelism and more about the conversational experience. Even then, it is possible that it would not be received well. But I think that somewhere in the mix, the dare of it could be appreciated, especially since some people have not been able to go to church like usual.

Those are all actual ideas that I have but lack leadership skills to implement myself. One other church or school program idea I will mention is the idea for a creative comedy or jester type hobby program, like a circus club, where young people can learn things like juggling, how to make animal balloons, yoyo tricks, card and magic tricks, and some basic joke telling fun. Also, there could be a skill-building food component of cotton candy vending, sno cones, nachos, caramel apples, and slushies. The idea would have to do with good-hearted humor and the knowledge could be used later in life if people wanted to make money doing animal balloon art or birthday parties or something. If a church used this idea, there could be a curriculum for learning about how to treat people well and be encouraging. A good final talk could include a description of when Jesus was mocked on the cross.

I decided to mostly list out regular ideas that could be used in churches or schools, or apartment networks, possibly because that is the type of participation that I am most used to. There is a ministry called "Metro Kids" in NYC that seems excellent but I think that with a lot of this thinking, I am really most motivated to simply get people the food they need just so they have food, or directly provide the religious component that some people have missed out on, and to do it in the most overt, straightforward way possible, with no hoops and loops of any sort.

Thank you so much for this amazing class and experience. I appreciate so much being included and I feel renewed in hoping to help make a difference through food and church service, especially keeping the Black church in mind and everyone needing more fair food practices.

Here is a chart that has to do with predestination:

Trilogistic Chart of Innocence

garden	cross	Judgement Day
discipline	forgiveness	unconditional love
Father	brother	mother
innocent of the crime	calls a lawyer from jail	found not guilty
Jesus	loves	you

That We Would Be Called Children of God

Something on Judgement Day that I am not looking forward to is seeing snakes crawl out of my mom's soul in front of everyone, and seeing my dad's grief as he is confronted about his own role in her unrelented abuse of me and psychological dependence that she convinced herself was okay. All of us there at the dreaded day of reckoning will feel the same as we do now, totally unsurprised yet horrified as we sort through the video footage and narrative documentations of the life scenes that turn out to have black bats and rabid pterodactyls flying through each infested backdrop once the spiritual-filter is applied and the whole reality is apparent. It will be literally dangerous to view the footage of my early years working at barnes and noble, with actual pythons and vipers emerging from the screens and snapping and lashing at all of us conferencing there at whatever Judgement Day location somehow exposes what people refused to deal with on earth. We will go through each segment of recorded evidence, dodging snakes with slitted eyes and giant fangs dripping with actual still-potent venom, probably re-biting and killing some of the friends and neighbors there with us who I thought were safe from additional Satanic attack. I will say, God, my sister already got stung by a jellyfish at the beach one time. I could hardly bear to see it. Can't that be enough? But it wasn't enough on earth, so why would I expect it to ever be final later on. That is why as part of whatever group of Presbyterians I am assembled with in the horrifying haunted-wilderness-nightscape-welcome-center to eternity, I already know that I will have to rely on my prepared consolation of saying, "I knew we were wrong all along." My preserved doubt will be like the lemon jolly rancher I found in my pocket on the hike back down from Mt. Mitchell as a kid, which was too long of a hike anyway, just like our other trips through the mountains erroneously claimed by the Scotch-Irish, who found their way to South Carolina after becoming too proud that there were no more snakes in Ireland.

All the Jews will be Saved

Well, already another blog post after quite a doozie about purgatory. But I want to mention a Bible verse that I find very assuring and that is a verse that says "All the Jews will be saved." I forgot where it is in the Bible and I do not care about the context. I don't. I just simply believe it and have hope. But I also know that Jesus Christ is the only savior and the only authority who has essentially made it allowable for anyone to be considered Jewish if they want to. That is why the Old Testament is part of the Bible. I also simultaneously believe that no one will be saved without faith in Christ. Well that is where it gets confusing, because one of the great gifts from Judaism is the fact that the Jewish people kept their faith as it is for thousands of years and many have maintained loyalty to that without converting to Christianity. I think some of the answers to the apparent conundrums can be found in the way Jesus died with a sign over him that said King of the Jews. His power to save his people no matter what they believe may have to do with that identity held on to until the end. The other thing I have to wonder is if some people will lose their Jewishness if they refuse to recognize their king. Well I don't know, and presbyterian predestination theology might line up with the idea that they don't have to because he recognized them first, and catholic purgatory theology might suggest that of course they eventually will, and waiting until they actually see it is what keeps it real. Well way to go everyone, I might be Jewish myself but probably only got included in Israel as an after thought trailing from God's eternal being.

This is Why I am Catholic

Ok everyone, it seems that it is time to discuss the concept of Purgatory. Why do I sometimes believe in and make plans for purgatory? Presbyterians generally believe there is heaven, hell, and earth, which includes a strict and ordained time limit to experience saving faith in Jesus Christ, without whom no one will be saved from a just and thorough punishment for sin, possibly in a way that lasts for eternity. I veer from some of these perspectives sometimes by suspecting either that a more final death as a punishment is possible, which would be like a type of annihilation, or that redemption is still possible beyond the grave. I have had to make room for those possibilities in my mind because of caring about hundreds of millions of other sinners who do not believe the same things that I do, and who often don't seem as bad as I am! How can I account for continuing problems in my own life after a definite faith in God, confirmed by now in many ways from the Holy Spirit, and especially how can I tolerate seeing millions of people I care about permanently, horrifically, and irrevocably choose what amounts to perpetual agony forever, all the while being told to alleviate suffering on earth as much as possible. What I most can't get around has to do with believing that death itself is probably not likely to be the automatic or even most common gateway to final righteousness for anyone. People do become clean and righteous in this world, which continues to be imperfect while we live out our lives, so how could anyone assume that what is right after death is automatically perfect, even if people immediately see Christ and are cleansed because of it? Most people know they face a reckoning for sins in some way after dying, so who is to say that it will be a totally happy experience? The Bible actually says there will be tears, and maybe the fact that they call it Judgement Day instead of something like a Year of Jubilee means something in terms of the process and timing. But God says a day is like a thousand years to him and a thousand years like a day. So I do not mean to make anyone lose their hope of immediate relief in any way, because the Bible does promise total eternal joy for all believers in Christ and not necessarily for anyone else at all. However, as an evangelical with a severe scrupulosity OCD, I have found that occasionally embracing almost any belief from Catholicism, including the possibility of millions of years of purgatory, puts me in theology territory where I see a whole new world of justice and opportunity that makes me pray with hope and love for anyone. I am still a fundamentalist of many sorts, but I want to present this purgatory idea to help other people who are in constant torment caused by not really knowing what will actually happen to people in God's presence, which might be part of life now more than we realize. I do not suggest it as an alternative to trusting Christ alone, but while we experience earth and suffering for whatever reason, the concept of purgatory can be a useful mental health strategy to find middle ground that could very well turn out to be a true and obvious reality dearly bought for us by the greatest mediator ever, Jesus Christ, who died and rose again to welcome any friend needing salvation.

Eternal York T-shirt

Ok everyone here is the t shirt I made. Do you guys think I crossed any lines with it? I think it is a cool shirt and I am excited about wearing it sometimes. It is true I might start a club and then pass out tracts and communion sometimes in various locations. People might assume that would be unauthorized but I am not sure it would be. After this post I will probably go back to my normal worldly monk posts, though I might add in some bible opinions sometimes like commentary that is different from theology ideas or christian life strategies. if you have not read the bible much before I will tell you my favorite book which never gets old and that is the book of matthew. Most people say to read the book of John first but I like the sermon on the mount which is Matthew 5-7. Genesis is also awesome and Revelation which is freakishly similar to the point where I have wondered if the beginning of the world and even the big bang is in the future and it creates a time loop where everything starts over. People in Genesis live for about 700 years and what if that was from health advances in the year 3000. Isaac Asimov suggests a similar idea in his story called The Last Question but it was presented for fun as a story so he might not get in as much trouble as me. But I am not going to get in trouble at all because of Jesus Christ and that is why I go ahead and do some crazy stuff like make t shirts that possibly only I understand.

A Very Indulgent Culture

Hi everyone, I hope you had a good Christmas. I want to share an idea that might seem obviously wrong to a lot of people, but actually might be just what some people need. And the idea I have is that I think churches should just go ahead and start selling communion. Probably for about a dollar until it makes people feel too bad to do it any more. Some will read this as satire, but it is really the opposite extreme based on perceptions from a difficult path through experiencing people being mad and mean for no reason almost all the time.   I just think for a lot of people who don't know better, "communion for sale" would be close enough to accepting God's free gift of eternal life, and for the people who do know better, the disrespect of it would be the irresistible grace they need to be saved from further crimes against the religious people they so publicly have despised. Do I need to go on and on about theology and church history? Probably not. I am tired of trying to figure out what time period this really is, with people always wanting to play holocaust with real lives, or accuse everyone of being part of the confederacy if they call out northerners on their hypocrisy. And I think for churches who really are guilty of manipulating people and creating weird economies where everyone acts like salvation is free but then wants you to pay them back with the misguided admiration that they are really after, then selling communion could help them, too, by being the more honest expression of their intentions.

Bible Study

You can understand what is in romans without reading it. basically people have different value systems but everyone has messed up based on what they know is right. but when paul says you are only held accountable for what you know, he refers to "the" law and not "a" law. but i think "the law" could also include science and be broader so it is one law. but our knowledge is partial anyway so if people want to view it all as different belief systems they can to some extent but everyone has violated their own belief system.

But the question is, what if people have a belief system that is all bad. well wouldnt violating that be like saving faith. like they are bad but made a mistake and were accidentally good one time. well people say being good one time isn't faith. it is just a random act of failing at the destruction you wanted to cause. so that is the doctrine of total depravity. if there was something that seemed good after all then the person finds out how to make it a loss by their final rejection that is like an ingratitude so bad that it would cancel that inconsistent moment anyway. that is my guess about it though really i would suspect that the mistake to be good would catch everything else on fire, destroying the evil and leaving only a saved soul who loves much because they have been forgiven much.

Things That Make Me Feel Cross

Ok everyone I have been reflecting on my faith experiences and remembering finally understanding the main thing I was tripping over about forgiveness of sins. Basically in my mind when I thought of Jesus on the cross, I could only see the crucifixion and not the atonement. So I could believe that the crucifixion happened for my sake, but I did not see the atonement that was also happening on the cross, which had to do with Jesus pleasing God on our behalf. The thing that was happening more than Jesus dying for me was that Jesus was pleasing God for me. So I could even take the cross out of it for a while and think okay, I was supposed to feed five thousand people and I only fed 287. But Jesus fed 5000 so things will be fine. God will say how many people did you feed. I will say 287. God will say, that is fine.

I can see how people could then say, no, it was also his death. he had to die and it was both his life and death. And i agree, but I think it is a trap for people to accidentally put their faith and trust in Roman execution. That is really a problem that I think is more common than people know, and to try to live by it causes a crucifixion experience instead of a happy life pleasing God. But in heaven all of it will probably eventually turn to life and atonement for anyone who asks or believes at any time.

Combined Blog Posts

The first idea is something I figured out which is that if people want to be humble, one really good strategy instead of trying to feel bad about yourself is just to pay attention to what is true all the time. You tell the truth and look for the truth and try to see things as they are and understand stuff. It helps people be humble because the fact is that we have no reason to be arrogant. So if instead of just trying not to be arrogant, you take an approach where you get to know people and love everyone, the humility happens more automatically. And you actually sometimes end up feeling more positive about yourself in an acceptable way.

Okay the second idea is about the verse that says God hates dishonest scales. It has to do with bad business practices which is something that abounds in our society. And the thing I have to say is if dishonest scales are bad, just think about how God feels about unfair algorithms and child trafficking. He is not happy with that. It is weird to me that some people don't care if God likes them.

Ok the third thing has to do with mindfulness and Jesus being a carpenter. He was making creations of wood and that is very temporary and present moment oriented. I think that is important. But then he became a healer doing miracles in his community. And the cross itself which was made out of wood took on some severe permanence in many ways. But what does it all mean in terms of eternity? Jesus gave people eternal life which to me is even further down the spectrum from rock and wood and more into a zone of water and spirit. But it also says Jesus is the rock where people can hide. So that is interesting.

Finally I will get into mental illness territory and say one more idea which has to do with the trinitarian nature of nature and important elements of oxygen, hydrogen, and carbon. To me those are the main three things. Hydrogen and Oxygen can be water or fire, and Carbon is the main element of life which is combustable as coal or can be like diamond material. And the Bible talks about a crystal throne in heaven. Well what if that crystal is carbon, and it refers to the human nature of Jesus Christ. So the crystal throne might refer to God's heart which is happening all the time everywhere so we don't wait until the book of revelation to be loved. Welcome to Kook Church Central, based on the love of God from the life of Jesus.

Why I Am Sometimes Genuinely Not Grateful

Ok everyone, time to try to focus on other things besides the horror of seeing what stage I am in as part of the torture re-enactment that seems to be starting over. I do not agree with these therapy philosophies of re-experiencing to try to achieve the lost mastery. I believe in replacing the trauma with positives, and I had plenty of stuff going for me that could have served that purpose. There is really no choice except for me to just be patient with it, although there are a few different options for quitting. That is all I have to say for now and hopefully I will be able to eat some food today and take a lonely unsafe walk through my rude neighborhood.

I am adding some more thoughts about this topic later, which have to do with the way I don't even know if the problems I feel from bad people are torture treatment or not. It could be from people actually being as bad as they seem to be, with my erroneous assumption that it is meant for my benefit in some way. But I maintain my conclusion that I think it does not benefit me and that there was a path of success that could have helped a lot of people and was prevented on purpose multiple times for political reasons.

However, some of the absurd obviousness of the harrassment and stone cold rejection that I experience makes me see a possibility that people have intervened to try to rebuild my patience that was repeatedly torn up to the point of brain damage. And it must involve a lot of generous participation, because thousands of people have been mean to me in recent years, with some rejection coming in more official ways from whole organizations. So I don't really know what the truth is, except to say I think general kindness and even common assumptions that being nice to people helps them heal comprise a far superior recovery strategy than to create a supposedly controlled re-traumatization. I just don't believe in that strategy and think in these times it is especially dangerous for that to get mixed in with the racism and other political problems that affect clients. Many mental health workers already find themselves in a conflict of managing activism that targets groups of enemies combined with professional responsibilities to help those very same people. And how convenient it is if "helping" them involves tearing them to shreds in the way their abusers did so they can practice standing up to it next time. Except they never should have had to stand up to it, and perpetually standing up to bullies isn't supposed to be the solution. Bullies shoud be stopped and good people should go about doing what good people do, which is treating everyone how they would want to be treated.

Anyway, the spiritual people in the background who see their role as supporting the opportunity for people like me to reach the next levels of forgiveness instead of successfully contributing to the much more useful work effort in a social and economic crisis will also turn out to be part of a torture dynamic if they can't see the insult of rewarding something like the happenstance of a gender identity malfunction while disincentivizing years of faithfulness, prayer, and honest work.

What am I talking about? Possibly it is too specific to refer to on a blog. And yet it is all too familiar to probably anyone. This concludes my begging for it to all stop, and if I can't find references for my peer counseling aspirations easily enough, I will be moving back to Greenville as soon as I can to face a nicer brand of torturers. I just didn't know how good I had it when people ruined my life in the first place.

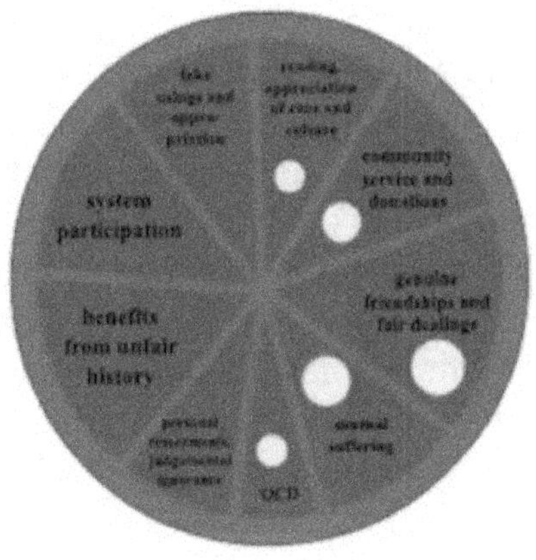

Racism Pie Chart

bad slices: systemic, privilege from history, appropriation and betrayal, personal discrimination and ignorance
good slices: education and appreciation, service and giving, friendship and justice, mutual suffering

other: OCD

Well everyone, this post is a little out of the ordinary, but I want to share something that really helped me have a more reasonable picture of my own guilt and innocence in regards to racism and the accusations that are mixed in our culture. I am very affected by it and have had to face the issue a lot while navigating life in New York City during social work school, volunteering, and living in my neighborhood where I am a minority but still part of a powerful majority in the surrounding culture of United States, at least so far. Racism can be as simple as not discriminating, or it can be as complicated as a whole economy and history.

Anyway, it has driven me crazy as I constantly either mentally defend myself, change allegiances in my mind, manage mental illness symptoms, and try to avoid hurting people.

So I just wanted to share a tool that helped me not keep blaming myself for all the world's problems in an irrational way.

This is adapted from CBT pie chart ideas that help people avoid "all or nothing" logical mistakes and "black and white thinking." I think some people have had to think literally about black and white for all their lives and they want for other people to also have to deal with the racial suffering. So in a way I will gladly take my share of it, but in another way, I think I have to literally draw the line and say okay, I am not going to throw my life away because of guilt and I am going to try to find some sanity in my life and social participation.

So I made a racism pie chart for myself, to see where I am bad or good, and to try to get at least a snapshot of a view that is more complex than just thinking I am bad or good, which usually makes me feel pretty bad.

The yellow dots are just on the sections where it is positive things that can help people. For this chart, you can see that I am probably just over the majority line in terms of being better at helping than hurting, though the OCD slice could sometimes be a problem instead of a good sign of caring about how my thoughts affect other people.

I don't think this chart is exactly representative of me but it is a sample of how people could assess themselves and see that really, racism probably is a major problem that needs to be personally fought against as much as possible every day, but also is part of a complex life where goodness is bound to prevail.

I just want to say, too, that is chart is not exactly accurate for me and just an idea that I am sharing for other people who might have some more extreme slices in either direction as the ones I have mentioned in this chart.

One other thing to notice about it is to think about which things are the things I have control over. I have a lot of control over thoughts and judgment but not total control. I have a lot of control over what I read and media but not total control. I do not have much control over history but I have some say in what I do with my benefits from it. I have some control of system participation but some is kind of forced compared to how some of the good slices would shrink if I refused to participate by going to jail or killing myself.

I think the slice I did for resentments and ignorance is actually a bigger percentage than what I have in real life but I think this ends up being kind of the defining slice where people really need to try to overcome that side of themselves while working hard to expand some of the other positive slices.

Way To Go, Everyone!

Congrats, Black lives Matter, I am so happy for you guys to get nominated for the Nobel Peace Prize. I think it is also a great ideological advance for people to see some of the force and war factors of true peace. So way to go. Some people are sitting in jail right now for it. However, I still don't respect that middle-aged middle-class white guy in Seattle blowing a leaf blower in cops faces. That disgusts me and so does a lot of the political racism in some of my environments that have truly damaged my race relations and hurt a dear and precious gift of friendship and happiness to live life with black people and other races too. But I am so happy and thankful for everyone who stands up for each other in this very dangerous and oppressive world.

Is this the time to mention another mad blog topic I have in mind which has to do with how unresonant the term "systemic racism" sometimes is in my ears? I just feel like a lot of systemic problems are sometimes more specific and varied in their targeting that transcends race, and calling it all racism too hastily sometimes allows the bad things to continue happening. An example is that I have a friend who truly believes she is better off avoiding most vaccines, including the Covid vaccine, and she and some other hospital workers know in their hearts that they would rather risk getting the disease than take a shot that was developed in a panic. I don't see it like that, but I do see what her hospital is doing by saying that she and the other workers refusing vaccines have to wear the masks that are M-100s, which basically look like old fashioned gas masks. The N-95s would be fine and everyone knows it, but the hospital system, called "Prisma," which already took over our town, is using the masks to shame people into feeling forced to get the vaccine, and it is also obviously setting these people up to be targets for patients who will say they prefer the workers with normal masks. It is something I am personally familiar with where the threat of job loss is used as a stress weapon to fight people literally TO THE DEATH. They are trying to kill my friend and it is that simple. These policies and system assaults often have some

intentions that aren't necessarily race-based but something else that
has to do with beliefs, values, and power. And honestly I find it to
be a betrayal when places like social work schools won't tell the
truth and instead simplify things in one direction so they can accuse
categories of people who they think opposing will make them seem
more innocent of their own racism sins. Should I go on? It has to do
with some principles of truth and people reaping what they sow. Do
you know who has planted some serious seeds of actual work in this
world lately? Chinese people and China as a country. That is all for
now. There is a lot more to say about people choosing their various
forms of work and investments, and decisions to block other people
instead of reaching out sincerely to those who lack
resources. Atheism could be part of the problem, or could not be,
but when people think no one is looking and no one will notice if
they try to reap someone else's harvest and get away with it, the
foolishness will always find its way back where it belongs, and God
will insure that credit goes where it is due. In the case of Black
Lives Matter, I would say it is a triumph of that very fact and people
who tried to steal from that effort or ruin it and give it a bad name
have been defeated pretty thoroughly. And the cops who did what
they were supposed to in all the crazy scenes will get their reward as
well. So way to go everyone, I am glad to have supported somewhat
and to have done so in such a minimal way that I still get to sit in my
warm apartment drinking coffee instead of suffering in prison for up
to ten years.

Complex Trauma

Hi everyone, I have some very rude posts up on this blog now, and I wanted to add one more simpler section to say that I do plan to support Medicare for All and think another long over due healthcare solution has to do with employers needing to pay people through actual wages and not group insurance. That is the main part of the leveraging scam that hurts everyone, and a private health care system should mostly be comprised of individual insurance sold directly from companies with no health-based discrimination. I think it could still work financially, and people should also be able to sign up for medicare until they can afford private insurance. It is an idea similar to Obamacare but without the group factor that those lawmakers knew people would not let go of yet. But the continuation of that system for now what must be thirty years too long is an abomination and a disgrace. And the fact that there yet remains another American system where people are treated worse, which is the legal system and privatized jails, is something that I almost can't believe. People talk about denial, but my experience with insurance genuinely does make it hard for me to believe that other oppressed groups have it worse and that there could be another system more intent on murder and torture. A lot of people have spoken out about it, yet still seem a little too dependent on the corporate money behind it all. Many so-called social justice politicians have been all too content to just take the money later from out of control companies and give it to the people who find themselves outside of the glob of exploited working people. Some of those outsiders are victims, but some are the worst of the oppressors and people's refusal to acknowledge that is part of the problem. I believe there are still solutions and if people do what they are supposed to and look for the true actions that benefit everyone, resisting temptations to choose fake, ideology-based temporary and one-sided non-fixes, then most people could start to work their way out of a very bad crisis that is costing many lives daily.

God probably doesn't love Joe Biden

I will go ahead and call it everyone, though we all know it, don't we. No, really, I am just joking, of course, sure I am, maybe God is not mad and the timing of the virus that happened right when the two presidential candidates essentially became biden and trump doesn't mean that our nation has lost God's blessing. God has obviously still taken care of us so kindly and thoughtfully by providing some of the things like zoom calls, food shipping, covid heroes, and I would say even an election of what probably actually is the lesser of the two evils that our nasty horrible culture inevitably wound up with.

But I will say it out loud as part of my lamentation about my own culminating problems from lifelong abuse at societal levels, family levels, church levels, and most thoroughly, health care woes. People found a darwinistic competition for survival to be their preferred way of handling the increased health and stress problems in our society, which only got worse, and people like me ended up with severe mental illness and the impossible task of keeping insurance for it. I am well past a state of losing everything, and yet it has gone on and on. But I don't think any of it can go on much more for me, and I might be at the point where I simply don't get any more health care for my problems and just let myself die.

I am complaining based on finding out yesterday that my medicaid got interupted for the second time, which means I will probably lose my other insurance that qualified me for a program to help me be a peer counselor and apply for housing at a reduced rate as a disabled person. It was a life that I was still stupidly looking forward to, even as part of an outrageous employment injustice that continues after years of work I have done to contribute to my society in any meaningful way.

I still cling to some dwindling hope that I can sell my e-books of work I know should have been sold about ten years ago and possibly before that. There is a delay because of lack of support, either from a slow, bumbling, backward Christian segment that still won't use my pen name properly, or the hostile, aggressive northern markets that I reached out to, who loved me in some ways but still refuse to fully back me because I don't match their disgusting, power hungry "out" required gender politics. They have carved out their religion as the exact opposite of my own background, like the inverse photoshop wand that selects any belief that opposes the religious people who got on their nerves. So they will help me as a writer, once I have sold or lost everything and agree to use my lifelong gender suffering to their advantage as a pawn.

And then, after I go ahead and compromise everything as part of my chronic ethical dilemma of staying alive when there is nothing but abuse for me in this world, I still have to call my sister and give her the bad news that my family's four hundred thousand dollar investment to help me escape the mistreatment of the south was all for nothing.

Sure guys, I will do that this morning, and just please email me the script of what to say and do next without ever gaining the freedom I have worked for. I know that my suffering that basically consists of all my organs slowly failing because of brain damage from chronic emotional abuse will actually still be nothing compared to what we see unfold for the next generation as other countries attack us and try to complete the assault on young people that has already been well underway and spearheaded by our own media enterprises such as the New York Times and Hollywood. Abortion and rape are their goals, and there are millions of people from other countries waiting to join in and pounce on our ruined country.

Congrats especially to the British empire for its own completed mission and actually rather successful outreach to the world, now fully accomplished and commemorated by the undeniable finale of American society being slowly or not so slowly martyred. Some of it, of course, is not martyrdom, but just regular old death, complete with moral decay, financial devastation, and literal disease. People still seem to have hope that they can get into the history books by squawking in the streets, but a society to read those books may never be found again, except in heaven, where people know better anyway. Some will insist they are not part of colonial conquests, but many of those people are actually the most integral and always have been, so way to go everyone, it is almost over.

Political Racism

Well, everyone, it's snowing, but thankfully the faithful workers at CVS were still there today so I could buy some medicine and apple juice. I did not see any marshmallow bunnies yet for Easter, but that can only mean that a bigger shipment is on the way. Another nice thing is that the cashier let me have a plastic bag for what I bought, which is something that doesn't always seem available now because of the new laws in NY forcing everyone to use paper bags. The law hit everyone right at the same time as Coronavirus, and I remember awkwardly trying to carry home some groceries in thin and tearing paper bags with no handles after braving the outside world during my first quarantine. It made me contemplate the eternal destiny of environmentalists whose control tactics and self-righteous guilt manipulation sometimes reminds me of Cain's rejected vegetable offering in the book of Genesis. Really, you won't believe that story if you read it, which is the main problem anyway, and the similarity of Cain's failed attempt to cover up a lack of true sacrifice is often on my mind when I see people smugly base their odd spiritual snobbery on vegetarian habits, organic milk that hasn't been properly pasteurized, and fake recycling programs for children who actually would do great just to learn about trashcans. People seem to think that hemp wallets and soap that doesn't work will secure their universal role as cartoon heroes who saved the world. Well God has said that he is going to destroy the planet and all the bad people on it, so I wonder who will be found opposing him in the end. Honestly, it probably won't be kind animal lovers, and yet you can kind of see some of the hell-oriented jihadist behavior when people burn down their own homes and habitats with wildfires for political influence instead of creating irrigation to save koalas, and when people vote to block oil production so whole economies collapse and children starve. The targets they are after is southern poor people who thought they were supposed to work for a living. This persecution is getting old now, like the democrat's sour milk of silencing rejection poured on our heads at the racist diners of segregated twitter followings on social media this past year from an army of blue Hazel Masseries.

Violence is Violence

Well that was quite an orange fire that raged for four years, put out by a mostly friendly blue ocean wave, but I think that as the steam hisses and people trudge through the charred wasteland to determine what can be salvaged, something that will turn out to be much less flammable than expected is evangelical Christianity. During recent days, some people in surprise occurrences of political integration have started testing christian claims of evangelical identity, looking for whether people actually share their faith or just found themselves as part of a popular and maybe comfortable social club that seemed immune to some of the suffering felt by oppressed and alienated groups. But that is where I and others will probably have to draw certain lines with how patient to be. Surprising to some, these lines may not be the bad lines of gerry mandering in voting districts, or pipelines through indigenous territory, or even Wal-Mart lines that were always too long on purpose. But they will be confrontational and supernaturally unchallengeable boundaries where our persecutors are faced with our unanimous outrage at their own hypocrisy of silencing us and then calling us silent. People love the MLK quote about the appalling silence of good people, a little too much, in fact, and not coincidentally enjoy even more the sport of comparing faithful Christian patience to the horrific silence of the Holocaust, famously brought to attention by Elie Weisel and others since then. People who question complicity in these matters usually have the best of intentions, which is to re-enlist the goodness of those they think they should have already been able to count on for defense against evil assaults on entire populations. But it is their own slouching when people demand the very moral compromises at the root of the problems themselves from people who do plenty of what they are supposed to and know it. What do people say they wanted from us. The criticism was of a lack of campaigning. And yet we were already muted for that very reason: the fact that we actually believed that people needed to know something and went to the trouble of being associated in any way with the message. So either people really believe we are wrong, and are about to be surprised sooner than anyone realizes when God comes through for his people, or there could be a second category of people who were secretly us and would not admit it. And in that case, I will say to those people this new famous quote: "when you point a finger, you have three more pointing back at you, plus my two middle fingers now too."

Channeling Self Harm

Well everyone, I hope you all are having a good night. I need to take my psychiatric medicine and try not to have another day where I scream at everyone in my neighborhood to stop torturing me. I have made good progress in life goals, which used to involve writing and publishing, but then just writing, and now just experiencing the humiliation of Christ and God's jealousy and rage from the Old Testament. There is oddly one more thing that I have figured out, which is a related goal to stay alive until the very end and not commit suicide. That is something I did not notice about Christ on the cross, not automatically as a suicide theme but that he was alive while dying in an unusual way. So I will try to do the same. Abandoning my more absurd and grandiose ambitions to not be abused by my entire society seems like a good plan for now and definitely a type of spiritual progress. It still might be a culminating problem, though, for people who will be found hitting themselves in the corner when my books are finally read in heaven. Probably already there are already creatures and people in other realms reading about everything we do here and who possibly have hologram machines that create physical replications of us that they can slap when anyone does something stupid. It could also be God's plan for me to fail in many life layers at a time, because he knew I was going to tell evangelicals that their communion might as well be fetal blood after their disregard for people's health care needs, and that I would also tell the democrats that their fetal blood might as well be fetal blood. Speaking of blood, I am thinking about having my gallbladder surgery without the pain medication or anesthesia, just as practice for the war.

[23] And you, Capernaum, will you be lifted to the heavens? No, you will go down to Hades. For if the miracles that were performed in you had been performed in Sodom, it would have remained to this day. [24] But I tell you that it will be more bearable for Sodom on the day of judgment than for you."

Now Things Can Go Back To Normal

Finally, some "peace" and calm again. No more yucky photos of that bad person on the news every day and the headlines that make us feel like racism is going to win if we try to keep a job and pay our bills. Suddenly things are seem so sane again, and why is that? Is it because a mad man is not in charge and the so called fanatics he represents, or because the people tearing up our country got their way and are now allowed to tear it up from above and not below? Fascism or socialism, what a great choice for a country that used to try for liberty and justice. I actually do feel some relief and am especially happy about Kamala probably being a good leader, but I also don't plan to pretend I don't see a dynamic where people haven't caused on purpose half the strife they pretend to save everyone from. It's funnily not even just metaphorically similar to criminal behavior where someone has an actual gun to your head and promises not to hurt you if you just hand over the cash. Except it's more like, "we promise not to hurt you any more," which means something bad has already happened. Well that is interestingly similar to their narrative, hard to escape, but possible if you are willing to lose your career or participation in main social venues. I myself think there is a conspiracy, and knew not to vote for Trump, but also can tell when I am watching a skit set up for some entertainment purpose where people weren't satisfied with the corruption of hollywood and want to turn our whole reality into a nasty violent movie. I ended up with a pretty good role as a food volunteer, more exciting than just being an "extra," but sadly automatically still a racist villain because my ancestors believed in Jesus Christ. My life also comes with a debt that matches what other people got as their salary, but of course it is just a blessing to participate at all. Are the Oscars still a source of honor? To me it would seem by now that any of the winners would have to walk across the stage hiding their face in shame, but maybe that turns out to be part of the movie now too. A very clever ironic twist, and possibly a good sign that everyone will eventually get exactly what they vote for.

Shock and Dismay

Well, here we go. Inauguration Day and some executive orders that mostly seem helpful, except for a few that are pretty obviously dangerous and disrespectful. Apparently Biden appointed some random guy to help with outreach for evangelicals, but still includes as an executive order a reversal on the policy of no taxpayer funded abortions out of the country. How horrible. Has anyone ever tried to really work it out at all, and maybe come up with a funding system where the people who believe in that stuff can pay for it? They seem to be able to do the political fundraising to try to force all the people who don't believe in it to pay for it. So why not directly pay for the "medical care" yourselves? I actually support some medical service where people do controversial things but I think if people can't see the difference between emergency tragedy situations and a 50 percent abortion rate that control freak weirdos try to get religious people to pay for just out of spite, then there is a charade that too many people are going along with.

Recently in some volunteer situations where people were being mean to me and there seemed to be a racial pattern, I decided to use the word disrespect when reporting abuse that seemed race-based. It is just safer than accusing people of being racist when they have more prior support in that scenario. That is actually probably why people highlight racism as a main issue so much, because they feel their identity power, but an interesting thing happens when you choose an alternative word like "disrespect" to describe it. All of a sudden some of the other hate becomes apparent, like the disrespect in classrooms, the disrespect of thinking immigration policies don't apply to you but welfare should, and the war-like disregard of drug laws, often becoming a shield for worse goals of rape and child abuse. Well that is beyond the disrespect category, but sadly very related, and it will be interesting to see if the people calling for unity are really about peacemaking and reconciliation, or if it is just another layer of blatant dishonesty and hatred that people still think they will never answer for.

Facing Reality

Something popular in the north right now is to show an ugly picture of a white person next to a good picture of a black person. That used to be reserved for politicians but now is something that everyone can experience. I want to say that I disagree with it and feel sorry for people who have philosophically come to any conclusion other than the faith that everyone should be putting their best foot forward at every time. If someone being at their best wounds someone else, then probably the person simply should be doing their best somewhere else. And where might that place be? Perhaps it would include overseas missions, which is the goal most blocked by liberal academia and bad media for about 30-40 years. It is all over the literature, all over everywhere, and now multiple generations have been taught that any mission work is a type of violating imposition. Is that mistake worse than the similar bad treatment of minorities that some think they can cover up by switching their racism to white religious people, or by hiding the fact that that was also their target, and possibly their main target for years? I do not know. The people who end up helping the most will probably be the people who tried to help everyone and did what they were supposed to. That is something people have lost faith in, sometimes in despair, and many still believe that God might not really love and care for all the people who are wrong about politics. And many especially think that he won't come through for all his people and defend them against any attack, whether it is drug dealers raping whole towns or the media defaming their religion. But God won't need to use "bad light"/"good light" photography tricks when the whole truth is apparent, and the bad people can no longer hide their selfish, cheating, power hungry, perverse and child abusive strategies to ruin the lives of anyone who they saw as their rival for worthless societal attention. No one will have to humiliate anyone on purpose, and the only question is whether people's ugly faces will explode from shame or from shamelessness.

Idea for Facebook

Ok everyone i have an idea for facebook which is what if there was an announcement feature where people could post to most of their friends without depending on likes for more people to see some posts. This would help I think maintain some true friend factors instead of making the mix with media and ads turn all social communication into market driven systems that reward certain content instead of any or all actual things people want to share. It wouldn't have to be all of it, like old facebook, but it could be a feature rolled out as a schedule of days or a random lottery stock or a set amount based on friends or followers, or a ratio according to posts. That is an idea that I think could help restore some of facebook's old appeal that has been lost. It is definitely a challenge, especially with some facebookers using it for very competitive purposes, but there probably is a way to help most everyone benefit from it somehow and preserve the relationships that have actually lost a lot of the "organic" nature even when the posts aren't ads that can go to people's friends more easily than their own posts. I say this as someone who has run ads and I think obviously facebook is good for commerce. But there is a way that people are helping themselves to people's social lives not just without any compensation offered but at the expense of people not even having full access to their own friends when they want to communicate in the way that was set up when most people started using facebook and then depending on it almost as a utility. I think it could still work on the basis of consideration and not necessarily profit contracts.

One more thought is that if the sharing based on likes can be based on formulas and algorithms then it would not be that different to distribute "coupons" or "announcement quotas" enabling "all access friend shares" based on some other combination of factors that reasonable people would be likely to accept if it really corresponded to their facebook habits.

Shark Attack

Well everyone, I got a notice today from Barnes and Noble saying that their customers' info had been compromised, and everyone's purchase and transaction records have been leaked. I always had thought that was just a risk with the membership program but apparently Barnes and Noble thinks it is their business to keep track of everything that people buy but not be responsible if it is made public. My purchase history with them is pretty innocent, but I think that this is a reminder of how they leverage power with their cashiers and to try to stay in charge of community decency standards wherever their stores are. I think they are able to achieve a blackmail effect on their employees if anyone ever decides to stand up against them for any reason. They might think they can dirty all of our personal records, but their brand is the dirt, and even being an employee or a customer has an effect of instant confession at worst, and possibly an automatic exposure of their community assault strategy at even more worst. So I could say I am worried about people coming after me because of my name on receipts, but all that will come to light is how nice some of their employees and customers were, and how patient, to then be treated with nothing less than absolute sexual abuse meant to ruin our lives.

Trending

Well everyone, I am not going to make the most of this post, but I should go ahead and at least mention the topic. At volunteer work a couple of years ago, I was sorting coats at a coat drive and made a comment about how I always thought it was messed up how some people would just announce what colors would be cool for that season, like when people say, red and gold is what is going to be popular this year, or "it is time for everyone to eat avocado toast." I have just always thought, who do those people think they are? But marketing is good sometimes, too, and when I said it this lady meanly said, "that is their job." And it was like she knew I was on disability at the time, and she was implying that at least those people are not lazy bums riding the system like me. Well I must say that is a pretty nasty insult, and the idea behind it is that maybe because I have an illness or injury that keeps me from being able to work for a while, then I am automatically a worse person than anyone making any money at all, whether they are a contact tracer or a TSA person, or maybe even a prostitute, which to me isn't necessarily as bad as just an ordinary bad boss of some kind. But anyway, it is like I am automatically a tax collector by being on ssdi...okay… I see.. it is from taxes. I am a tax collector. Okay I get it everyone, thanks a lot for the great Sunday school lesson. To me that elevates you all to the highest of clergy even if you are one of the marketing people choosing what colors for people to like or deciding that it is time for society to have tax funded abortions and video ads in the subway depicting pre-teens in their underwear.

The Wages of Unfair Wages

Well everyone, in one of my other writings I said something that I think made it sound like I don't understand something that I actually do have a concept of, and it has to do with what is the opposite of slavery. And I just want to say in this quick blog post that a lot of education about slavery always compares it to freedom, like freedom is the main thing to be gained instead. But I want to say that I think wages might be the main thing, or an additional thing, and that some kinds of freedom come from having correct wages. We have problems like this now in our country, and people think it is okay, because they see freedom as the main thing in question, which ends up focusing more on the freedom to make people work without paying them enough. But wages might be the main thing, and the work itself is also a thing. Abolitionists who made slavery go away a long time ago didn't always offer other work opportunities, so a lot of poverty and suffering continued from American slavery while many people congratulated themselves and have felt innocent of certain atrocities. But work, wages, and freedom are all part of the justice picture, and people should consider this when they try to solve problems or assess how dependent they have become on other people's mistreatment. It's a lot to manage, and it is part of the reason why people should give all their effort to be a good person and do what is right. And not to make everything theological, but a related topic would have to do with something like tithing ten percent and thinking that excuses you from offering your whole life to the service of God and others. A lot of people will find that to give an honest ten percent, you kind of do have to give your whole life. And so many people have thought all of that is not worth their time. But probably almost everyone would be surprised at how much the other problems of percentages can be traced back to it.

Fighting the System When You Are the System

This topic is very belated, but everyone knows what I am talking about. I thought of a name for it, which I would say is "policy-mongering." It is when the lawmakers fight each other through the legislation process. And I think that it has been so much a problem that people should do what they always should have done and make it be against the rules. Not necessarily a crime, but just against the rules so you lose your job as a senator if you can't work in a straightforward process instead of using every aspect of the congressional system to fight "the other side" as a representative. The fact is, in that context, there is not supposed to be another side to that extreme, even with all the history of things like filibustering. Well filibustering also was a waste of time, and disrespectful, and people should not keep their jobs if they can't see their work as a job instead of a battle. There is something cowardly about blocking the other politicians at every step of government if what they really want is a war, though that doesn't necessarily mean that duels are the answer. Both sides have done it consistently, which almost makes it a treaty or agreement of some sort, and that is actually part of the problem. That is how it becomes a charade and sham while a whole country waits for justice. The right solutions would benefit everyone, and though the divided country and people who are not at peace with each other makes government a difficult challenge that is all too easy for someone like me to sit back and criticize, it is too much of a lie for people to say they are there to govern when what they are really doing is a much lower level role as a soldier taking orders from voters they are try to please in order to keep salaries and insurance that so suspiciously don't match the wages of the people who can no longer afford places to live.

When to Sort Things Out

People seem pretty mad about riots and looting that have happened in recent months, but that is where I see some of the people who are actually honestly fighting problems instead of doing weird power-play psychological lashes like what a lot of politicians, media, and other bad people do. It kind of matches how people always get in trouble for assault but other life-ruining strategies that happen all the time in this country are often tolerated and sometimes even legal. But I want to say that as people report on the Breonna Taylor murder, it seems that not everyone thinks it is important that there actually was a drug bust, and that probably her good life and herself as a good person had been turned into kind of a human shield by drug traffickers. I think there is a range of how bad drug dealers can be, but this sounded like pretty serious drug trade to me, and it continues to confuse me that people so much want to build a case against all cops but ignore the very bad abuse of millions of people, especially young people, from trafficking and drug attacks. A lot of it creates bad situations like what happened to Breonna Taylor, and I don't know for how much longer cops and soldiers need to be sifting through the complications of innocent people being mixed in before it just becomes a war. And if it does, then people who decided to flood the jails as part of that effort will have to face the consequences of their decision. For a lot of communities, it still seems worth the effort to try to intervene in trafficking, especially because of the international threats and the child abuse involved. And I can't say that I am not someone who thinks it does damage people's credibility when they want to talk about mass incarceration without acknowledging mass crime. I pretty consistently side with the black people and see a lot of racism, and I side with the poor and see abuse and lack of justice, but when I read the news, I see lies. You don't know how bad you have to be to lose my support, and many people have. I am not scared to become Amish, to go off the grid, and just wait until judgement day when God tosses millions into the yawning chasm of fire that is probably already glowing a little brighter from recent days.

The Green Blob

Well everyone, the conspiracy seems to be saying to do another blog post even though I just spent 8 hours blogging. So I am adding this post about how I visited one of my favorite hospitals this week to try to go to the Medicaid office. The hospital is called Metropolitan hospital, and when I went there, I was wearing a giant green coat, which is the exact color of most gallbladders, so I felt like I was kind of like a gallbladder mascot visiting the hospital. And people did seem cheered up that I was there. So that was really fun and I will think of them when I have my gallbladder endoscopy procedure that might happen soon. I am hoping that the endoscopy people will find the gallstone and take it out right then instead of just sending in a tube down my throat, into my innards and taking videos that I am sure will make their way to tik tok, possibly even before I wake up from surgery. Another joke I thought of to say in this post is something like this: Has anyone noticed that Dr. Fauci's name sounds kind of like Faust? Do you guys get that joke? It is like I am trying to say covid scientists are bad people trying to hurt everyone or something. But I don't really even know that much about what has been going on because I get my news from the latino soap operas on the TVs at the laundromat. When I watch the shows in spanish, I don't really know what is happening, and that is just like watching or reading the news online now.

By the Time Anyone Reads This I Will Be Drinking Coffee

hi everyone, I hope you're having a good Wednesday. Is Wednesday still hump day during Covid. I do not know. For me it is a good day because of some Reeses pieces and because I found the bag of brown sugar that I thought might have gotten thrown away in the shuffle of life. I'm also thinking of trying an experiment where I add some peanut butter to coffee with cream and sugar. I do not know if it will be a successful coffee flavor but it could be a good thing to try except for my gastritis and gallbladder problems, which may mean that I soon have a visit to the hospital, where I will mostly be complaining that they don't have peanut butter to add to their coffee there. But maybe they will. Maybe eating reeses pieces is part of the endoscopy procedure, much like swallowing barium at labcorp, with records that will probably show up on some tech site profile some day with some gossip from who knows when. Maybe I should just make a profile like that myself with all the worst case scenario info and then try to make my way in the world like normal and say it was a sociological experiment. All that would distract everyone from the actual mishaps, which maybe turn out to be not that interesting anyway. Well that is enough for today everyone. Don't forget to vote if you haven't already. We don't need four more years of really anything that you would find in the news on any day.

A Reading from the Cheese-o-meter

Well everyone, here is a little blog post for a sunny saturday. I just ate some yummy food which was simply some canned chili and rice. But what I did was combine a hormel can of chili with beanie weenie, which has more beans and is sweeter and has chopped up hot dog pieces. Well that plus some rice and a little bit of sour cream is actually very yummy. What about some cheese? Well I did not have any cheese this time. Not all of life is about cheese. Just joking. It actually is, but I simply did not have any cheese in my refrigerator. And the food was still yummy. So what have we learned. Well I don't know about you guys but I have learned to keep liking cheese but sometimes just drink a coffee if I already ate some chili and rice and sour cream and am just sitting here typing without that many good ideas to say. I mean what do you guys want me to say. Do you want me to say that the food wasn't that yummy? Well it was yummy. That is what this blog post is about. Life is about cheese, and this blog post is about eating some chili and rice without cheese this time. Honestly I am starting to feel a little persecuted. All I was saying was what I ate for lunch but I can tell from the awkward, rude, hostile unsaid accusations that people think I ate too much cheese with my meal today, when I clearly said that I do support cheese and simply did not have any in my refrigerator. Legal inquiries can be directed to (202)353-1555.

A Very Dave Thanksgiving

Well everyone I just posted a picture of Dave on facebook. Dave is my pet guinea pig and I was thinking about saying "Dave is the reason for the season." Which is partially true because it is Thanksgiving and I am thankful for Dave. But that might have made the photo go viral or even "pandemic" and Dave is not ready for that kind of notoriety. Dave is an excellent guinea pig and helped me get through Thanksgiving yesterday after I went through some stuff with indigestion and mental illness symptoms.

Roger and Fred, my other guinea pigs who died earlier this year, are celebrating Thanksgiving in heaven or maybe haunting houses if that is what they chose as their near final destination until the trumpets sound and guinea pigs are gathered from the four corners of the earth, etc.

It seems that I am in the mood to say things right on the edge of acceptability. Well that is where Dave and I reside along with a lot of mice and imaginary mice.

Have a great holidays everyone and save some turkey for me and Dave because we are planning to surprise a lot of people who wouldn't be expecting to find us at their holiday tables eating some food and telling everyone that facebook invited us to all their family gatherings.

Happy Day After Groundhog's Day

Hi everyone, I hope you are having a good day. I am doing okay and just trying to recover from all the groundhog's day festivities. Having a pet guinea pig means that you end up being the one to host most of the celebrations like posting a photo on facebook. Anyway Groundhog's Day is a nice low pressure holiday that doesn't usually hurt people, much like groundhogs themselves. Around Thanksgiving and Christmas, and New Years, and especially Valentine's Day, people often get depressed. And there are pressures to get everyone a present or show up at parties or go along with whatever social stresses there are. But with Groundhog's Day, you just have a conversation or two about whether the groudhog saw his shadow, and then everyone knows that it does not affect anything. Not even six months of winter.

I actually think there is some untapped potential with Groundhog's Day. Like for people to have a low key celebration of some kind, or just to shirk some responsibilities because of a holiday. One cool tradition could be for people to actually hide a groundhog in each other's apartments or homes every year. So people instead of just wondering that morning if one random groundhog will see his shadow, they will know they might end up finding an unexpected new pet that will need feeding and care for several years. Or at least until the next year when they hide the groundhog in someone else's house. Guinea Pigs could be close enough for this new tradition, or giant capybaras, like the Thanksgiving Capybara pictured here:

Gallbladder Mascot

A post on facebook said this dog does not like commotion or quick movements. Well that is how I feel so I am wondering if this dog is me but it kind of reminds me of my sister. So I really don't know but I definitely like looking at this dog more than the demons I see sometimes during hallucinations that are probably real.
 Currently I have to figure out how to get rid of a demon that looks kind of like Scar from the Lion King but with black and white paint and blond streaks and which was sitting on the operating table in my mind as I prepare for a gallbladder endoscopy. I think the demon is trying to tempt me to say something hateful to the people who caused the injury last fall. I remember when it happened, and a few weeks later my gallbladder was twinging, and a few weeks after that, it had steady pain and gallstone symptoms. But the doctors say they don't see a gallstone. So the diagnosis is gutwrench F.25 with gastritis and provocation, plus some Z codes that happen to be names of people. Some of the people are such nice people that I wondered if they hurt my gallbladder on purpose as a free referral for medical care. But what is more likely? It is more likely that I drank too much coke, and that I am tired of people hurting me.

Peeps is Easter Dinner

i gave those peer people a warning shot
which means i skipped two groups
because of gastritis
because i couldnt take it any more
because i decided to do the best i can.

rice and cheese and chicken soup
a little bit of mustard
against medical orders.

try to stay out of the e r
but visit if it is a day with
free jelly bean easter rabbit cakes.

pink bunny cakes like you saw on facebook
with easter grass but dont say guinea pig grass
because they will think you are selling pot
to that guy yelling at the people
to see who will say don't do that
or to see who will ask their mom
for a taser for their birthday.

now i have broken confidentiality rules
and will be sent to duane reade
instead of CVS
where you cant win in court against a covid hero.

that is why the socialists are taking over my neighborhood.

I owe the holocaust survivors 40 dollars
but it could go to the people
sending me emails to make it seem
like i went to their meetings
so no one will know who really did.

that is not right.
bad people gave me a membership card.

that is why i am going to
re-aim the drones from the new york times
and the thing i am not saying.

people thought there would not be a thing i am not saying
but i took my medicine a lot this week.

trouble in my neighborhood

In my neighborhood people block me as I walk down the street and then block each grocery in the stores and do power plays at the cash registers to try to make me beg them for survival and food and medicine. There are recordings of me complaining at Bank of America, where they won't cash any of my tax return checks, and at Duane Reade and CVS where they pretend to shelve something right where I am standing no matter what aisle I am in. Any way when the blocking is most blatant like when multiple people stand in front of you and pretend to have a conversation on the sidewalk or a group holds hands to try to make you break them or go around them, or when they actually touch you as a threat or make dogs noises at you, then it is tempting to say stuff back regarding harrassment or civil rights laws. But it is illegal in NY to say "illegal," and they know that so they try to provoke you. People in my neighborhood have now harrassed or threatened me over 10-15 thousand times. There actually was just a seminar about street harrassment offered by my old school but I did not go because I know that school supports these people instead of me because of my background as a good person. People are ashamed of themselves so they don't know what to do except make good seem bad. Anyway I am learning to manage my mental illness symptoms from other mistreatment and avoid saying things that could make me go to jail with all the foreign drug dealers using up tax dollars on purpose. So this is my translation key:

things to try not to say:

death and shame to you in the name of jesus christ
you're a bad person
I'll be sad when the militias gun you down
Dear Jesus help us kill them all
"is it legal to say this is a crime"

Safer things to say:

Hi Richard.
The Lord is not pleased.
I'm sorry Satan is raping your people.
any gibberish impression of their speech
Hey do you remember me from Nam?

I am sorry that I wasted the syrup I bought from the Amish on Amazon

Ok everyone I know that I have suggested solutions before that have to do with varying funds so that opposing political parties could pay for only what they believe in with clear consciences. But I thought of an idea this morning rather suddenly that I think could be a more obvious long overdue solution to all of it. And what I think could solve everything is if America just sent the whole bill for abortion costs directly to the Amish. They could absorb the disrespect intended for all religious people, much like Christ on the cross. It would be a powerful witness of God's forgiveness, while also satiating the murderous forces who try to abuse all of us in more sneaky ways. We could defeat them by just skipping to the ending, acknowledging the real goals, and concentrating all the meaning in a simplified form. And it is simple: people who care about doing what they are supposed to should take the punishment for everyone else. I mean just say it. There is no need for thousand page insurance laws and corrupt government gridlocks to disguise it all. People have not been able to convince anyone that babies are innocent or not innocent. But we know the Amish are, so let's get them involved a little more.

secret shoppers

i think there is clearly a problem with patience and yet it seems that might be exactly what is being targeted. to make me look compulsive and interpret it in a freudian lens of some sort. so some people are so nice but it happens to be at the same time where I figure out four or five things that I had worked towards are all tricks, which is after a series of about several thousand things just like it. And people say this could actually be helpful for everyone if you would just go along with it. And yet does it ever really turn out that way? I don't think so. It's not really a high level of ethics, either, like something advanced that the northerners would be guaranteed to figure out before anyone else. It is a simple choice: Stay alive to be tortured or kill yourself to help the next victims know that is an option for them too.

So maybe I just need to make a pros and cons list. But to know ahead of time that all the pros are really cons in disguise or will be at just the worst time kind of messes that up. And people say this is the whole argument, that you also already know that all the cons are pros, so instead of saying you can't win, then you say you can't lose. Except I would say, well then if one of the cons is suicide, then I'll choose that one and now it is the pro that accessed the other pros blocked on purpose. Now everyone is lost. People are saying well wouldn't you want double the pros? And I already said I don't think it works like that as much as you think it does. But do you know what does work really well? the suicide method in question.

an off the wall devotional for young people

Well everyone, some people lately have been sharing the lepsog
with me. What is the lepsog, you ask? Well I will tell you. L-E-P-
S-O-G. It is the opposite of the gospel. Basically it is when people
say you can't be blessed because you did some kind of defining
thing wrong or your particular combination of mistakes happens to
be the exact code that unleashed all the evil into the world. And that
seems to be what has happened with some of my lifelong efforts to
be productive. What else could account for this ongoing instablity
and disability and threats to lose everything even before it is gained,
always paying everyone a life savings to participate at all, with bad
things magnified and good things completely ignored if not
destroyed on purpose? Well some of us who have been patient with
lepsog tactics like that have found that we can defeat that kind of
evil by doing the unexpected, which is staying alive. So our lives are
full of secret messages that can be read backwards for some good
news. And some day, when people finally fight all the medusas who
have ruined this world, it will just take some mirrors to set things
right and access a great story to read about good people who did
what they were supposed to.

conditions

Well everyone, it is time for some friendlier blog posts and a little bit back to normal. I hope people in Texas are doing okay and I think all of these crisis situations in the past year or so will help everyone understand more about people's need for a generous and functional society. It could be that socialism will be the perfect bridge for future interaction and trade with communist China, which will hopefully wake up from the opium den of buddhism soon.

Anyway I guess I am still saying some crazy stuff that I kept to myself all this time of people's thirty-year spittle campaign betrayals inches from my face as I've tried different things to survive and participate in society. I have oriented a lot around a choice to stay alive even under conditions of moral compromise but the cost to keep me safe and surviving now without an income for writing or other work to me has far surpassed an amount that is appropriate for anyone to have to provide, especially under coercion of law or just my own guilt manipulation habits that developed from trauma and actually very legitimate outrage. I would say too that sometimes it feels like an insult for people to make a show of extravagant life support while rejecting hard wrought creative work that honestly was often between levels of either genius or miracle, transcending modern culture but full of enough foibles and failure to keep my whole life accessible and defeatable in a kind and friendly way. That is weird to be on this topic again but I say that as someone who has decided I might as well say what I think of people's little games for attention or money while priceless foundations bought with blood crumble away beneath everyone. Who am I talking about. I am not talking about people who have been nice to me. Some people say lentils in a good way as they try to save your life from the mercurious sharks. Some people say lentils in a bad way because they know you still like kellogg's cereal as an american and they want to replace that with their k-word agenda of karma, which is a fancy term for revenge on people who did nothing wrong.

Now where will this post go. My mad blog is getting blurred with my humor blog. That is not a good sign. It is a sign as bad as any zodiac sign or even the Zodiac killer. Do you guys remember that guy? I am thankful to not be him. It was not a given that I wouldn't be. I have truly managed a monster by controlling my thoughts and behavior, and stewarded a saint as well, which everyone has the opportunity for. Really I am thankful for what is actually a long life full of interesting experiences and people, who I think won't regret their efforts to help me but would probably share my frustration and hurt feelings at the way so many people have set up such bad terms and conditions in the territory of my mind and soul that they still underestimate and think they can get away with burying alive.

Raca, Fool, Nietszche

Ok so they are saying that the Enoch story could mean justice
already happens
but to me it could still be the tip of the iceberg for Enoch
and I would say an interesting case to look at
alongside that would be
Nebudchadnezzer who eventually did come around, didn't he?
So does he not get the whole works and if so are we going to say
the justice was in his cow days
or are we going to say
the justice is in the recording of his cow days
and does the recording ever go away, and if so,
then wouldn't the word be the will and the will
include a recording and an unrecording?
That is probably why letters are not the same
as ink splotches although they can be
in the computer world
that might fade
if other machines take over,
like squirrels and rabbits.
But anyway I genuinely don't know
but think people need to figure it out real quick
because that is why a lot of people think
that meditation is the same as prayer
which I kind of say in the next post
but of course don't really believe.

Questionable theology

Ok everyone. I just talked to a pastor at my church and I asked her one of my recent theological questions which is basically how much righteousness do we get from Christ. Like do we get our own righteousness restored and just get to be ourself as a good person after all, or do we get something infinite in some way, or do we actually get credit for saving people from their sins. That is where I would say probably not but that was what Christ's righteousness accomplished. I think this has to do with a concept called limited atonement which is a commonly un-agreed upon thing. And my pastor is a Baptist but she said that she thinks it might not be about credit. And I think she might be right and I might have been plotting to just get a paycheck from what happened at the cross. Well that is very rude and yet kind of a good idea and I already did apply to be a chaplain at a hospital so I could pray for miracles and then sell some kind of miracle tonic like the risperdal and trileptal that I was supposed to take to prevent these blog posts.

ok back to normal this time, i promise

My blog posts are getting mixed up now and I am inadvertendently becoming one of the bad people I tried to escape. I think I am rushing things a little bit and that is why I am messing up. I just feel a time pressure either from the apartment pest control situation where I got charged 2000 dollars and the problem isn't over, or because of my plans to commit suicide next month after figuring out that the torture is simply not going to stop. It is kind of funny to have kept thinking that it would for so many years. To have memories of explaining to a friend 15 years ago why I try not to say stuff about my mom even though she has problems, but then to have finally gotten to a point where that is all I write about. It is a dream come true except for any part of the reality whatsoever, which gets worse exactly proportionally to how hard I work to escape it. It is comedy that there must be some kind of audience appreciation for, like a slapstick show where I keep thinking that the next school degree will make me more marketable, or a job program can keep me safe from people's bullying, or a housing application will keep me from paying 3000 dollars for the cleaning company to organize one shelf and confirm as a legal favor that their gouging is how I get treated all the time. That is just what I needed for a trial that will never happen, and would be just another assault on anything and anyone I care about if it did. Some people bank on that kind of stuff more than I do, though, and for me I really kept thinking that earning a living was my ticket to earning a living. Like an almost foolish assumption that oranges come from orange seeds. But orange thiefs come from orange seeds in this world, and I can't afford to play the game any more. The conspiracy was such a good opportunity in some ways, and just the other day I was planning to do a blog post about a realization that patience was like a third vocational calling in addition to poetry and prayer. That is sweet isn't it, and a nice life. Poetry, prayer, and patience, with all the time for it that I could ever want. Except there is something else going on that has distorted it all, and that I can no longer tolerate, which is for

each hope to turn out to be the lettuce in a field of cabbage patch
demons. That was a good one wasn't it. I was trying to make up for
mixing the orange juice metaphor like a party punch spiked with
ginger ale and the detergent I try not to accidentally drink because of
my mind that got burned by literal harry potter fire at the bookstore.

Anyway, what I am saying is that I will be sad to miss whatever is
next in my life, or really in other people's life that needed me as an
epileptic bug zapper, and I especially will miss reading earth's
version of the daily news. I am sure that the next few years promise
to be as inspiring as when Obama rescued Otto Warmbler from the
North Koreans and when Kayla Meuller got what she deserved for
appropriating Muslims. What school is that from. No, take a guess
of who is behind me. It is the reason I can't be successful or stay
alive any further.
   My church agrees that about two more weeks should do it, and
then it is off to the next horizon, which probably will turn out to be a
painting on a brick wall that I crash into for some more
laughs. Would I be more motivated if I could see the audience? I
actually can. It's demonic portrayals like hologram distortions. I saw
one a few hours ago. It is actually a compelling reason to live once
you start seeing visions, but I don't have the funds for that kind of
lifestyle and don't intend to steal from people who already did
everything they could to either save me from torture or make it
worse on purpose. I can't tell the difference anymore after becoming
confused to the point that I am, which I think at its core is from
believing all the shocking accounts from other nice people who have
been treated in suspiciously similar ways.

adding this later- final wishes: please use my corpse in one of those
photos used to make white people look bad. thanks everyone for a
whole life like that, it was a great privilege

credits

 Ok everyone I am sorry for the outbursts in recent days but it is reactions to real things that people have done on purpose and my resolve to not let it affect behavior is actually not that strong because in some ways I think it should.

But anyway I think the hospital people will want to try to catch some demons on the EEG and it will be a fun time for everyone and the insurance and charity involved is not such an injustice to humanity that I should kill myself too early in this next phase of moderated harrassment and managed frustration or rage provided by thousands of people trying to help my judgement day stats.

So I appreciate everyone's work and I think these blog posts say some underexpressed views and establish my main grievance to all the torture which is the loss of my good behavior that I worked so hard to recover and maintain. And yet it is gone and I am just a bad person like people who didn't even try to do the best they could. But probably there was some level of assault on their lives too, so I will happily take my place with other humans in the same boat who will eventually have to acknowledge our relatedness as a formal club to play darts and pool table games together throughout eternity.

my neighborhood

the good news is
theres not a lot of gangs.

the bad news is
it's kind of all one big gang.

poem

I am going to copyright
blue rectangles
so that anyone who uses
that shape in a drawing
has to pay me 50 dollars.

Literary Edition

I think a good alternate title
for the Bible could have been
"A Very Special Whale"
because of the part in the story
with Jonah and the giant fish.

gice i would put that poverty next to anyones in the world and
people can try it themselves for five minutes and we will see who
would last it would be no one at all so have a great day everyone but
i am a lazy pig who spends too much but i did do the best i can and
if people want to say they advocate for anyone while ruining a life
like mine that could have helped everyone then they can have a
bloody mess pulp of intestines as their yearbook picture in heaven.

anyway among the mentally ill and probably some other suffering
people including jail there are probably some people who did stay
alive under certain terms but were they those exact terms all i can
say is probably not. and are all those people like that? nope. and all
the newspapers in the world won't change that so you can either
hump the furniture in front of humanity or start doing the best you
can every day which is a matter of one flicker of not being a total
piece of crap.

poem

what if there was a religion
where you just believed
anything anyone told you

poem

what are we going to say
when we get to heaven
and it's just Jesus
sitting at a very
powerful typewriter.

Disorder

The patient sat in the hospital. The doctor came in and sat down.

The patient wondered if the doctor had seen the part of the video eeg where she had put all the extra apple sauce in her book bag.

Well Refried, good news, you don't have epilepsy."

"That's great!"

"Just joking. You do have epilepsy and will need to have police supervision on the subway."

"Oh, well that is good too."

"And hand over the applesauce, please."

Before Refried could reach over to get the applesauce, the doctor got up and reached into Refried's bag and took the applesauce. Refried noticed that the doctor also took the cadbury egg that was in the bag from an earlier trip to the store.

The moral of the story is always do the best you can.

The Story of Ten Thousand Thunders

the character is named thaddeus james raddison of shropshire.

thaddeus is hoping to win a gingerbread house contest and figured out that it would be easier to construct the house with caulk instead of icing. He felt that this was kind of an ethical dilemma because he knew the judges always tasted the gingerbread houses too and factored that into the score.

Well a solution to that problem would be to include something so yummy on the gingerbread house that the judges would eat that instead of the caulk.

But he knew some judges would think that maybe they should eat something standard instead of something like a cadbury egg or whatchamacallit.

So he decided to cook something that the judges would think shouldnt be wasted, like a steak.

Thaddeus constructed a gingerbread mansion that took up as much space as some traditional doghouses, and added several stories of skyscraper sculptures on it. He ended up using a lot of office supplies and glues and cement caulks, as well as some sharp metal pieces to fortify some of the walls. Then he glued gumdrops and candy all over the house. Finally, he cooked a steak and used the spike on one of the skyscrapers and jabbed the steak onto the scene. For one of the store signs on the buildings he spelled out "shame to waste a cow like that."

Then he used a cart to take the gingerbread creation to the contest grounds. People set up their various gingerbread houses all along the display tables.

The judges evaluated all the creations and took tastes of candy and gingerbread from most of the houses.

When they got to thaddeus's mansion, the main judge took the steak off the spike and ate it. He said "I love steak, this was very creative."

"Congratulations Thaddeus. You have won the contest."

Everyone cheered and thaddeus won a golf cart.

soundtrack: "at the cross" on youtube

Yellow Phone Story

"Excuse me, can I has some cheese?"

"Milky, I can't believe it's you. Where have you been?"

"We took a trip to the Cloisters. It was grand and we spend forty ages doing cheese rep work in the condition valleys."

"That's amazing!"

"Thanks, Peabody, what have you been up to?"

"Well me and my brother are starring in a movie about a phone mystery."

"Really? That sounds neat!"

"Thanks. What happens is that there are some yellow phones against a wall. And one of them rings every day at four oclock. Well this schizophrenic guy thinks that he is supposed to answer the phones each day and do the opposite of what he is told. And the instructions always have to do with cooking some food and delivering it somewhere. Well it so happens that the schizophrenic guy really needs meals, so what he does is try to find some food that matches the description of what he is told to cook and he asks for it and says it is because of the yellow phones. Well the people always give him the food and a newspaper writes a story about how everyone went along with it and how the guy thought it was a miracle. Well then some people believe it and travel to the phones themselves and answer the phones and they find out that they all won a million game show prizes and trips and christmas extravaganzas because it was actually a miracle and the phones wires are directly from heaven and if you are reading this story you just won forty five million jackpots.

Theme poem thanks maria

jingle bell jing jang jangle bell jingle bell jing jang jangle bell hingle
hell fingle fell bing bang bongle bell times fifty if you try to do the
best you can then try to find a chili can from wal mart from target,
from someone's mom named margaret, i see a dollar found a dollar,
tried to holler stop the crop but then they figured out i meant another
thing i didnt say well then they play like try to stay and bring a bag
of sunny ray thats koolaid mix from what they fix in all the people's
wagon carts that line up near the streets of stone that weave into the
mountains and pass by all the homes where no rhymes are allowed
so people try to jsut sit calmly by the fires and eat some porridge
without bothering anyone but everyone knows that something is
causing the cave of misty sunloss to be pooling icy waters in a
whirpool much like the legends that were told around the stone
cricle complex meetings where the elders knew to allow youth to
say their ideas. One guy shared an idea for a new invention which
was a toaster that also charged your ihpone and the slots for the toast
and phones switched randomly intermittently so you never know for
sure if you are either about to ruin your iphone or find an image of
your facebook friends burnt into the toast like a miracle of
christmas. jingle bell jingle bell jing jang jangle bell jingle bell
jangle bell then repeat with jam and toast.

the innocence and the competency

What is needed is magic water to break a spell.

Antifa has to sign your social work license

or you can't be a Christian counselor

You think it's Africa but it's Mars

You think it's them but it's us

Trump is going to put Andrew Jackson

On every bill

which works out

If it means he has to pay for it all.

what is a jubilee

If not an explosion

Of jelly beans on easter.

using your noodle

 Well everyone, the secret messages seem to be saying to do a post about racism against Asians and I will gladly do that because I think it is a neglected topic. But I think at this point the main thing I will say is just to point out a simple fact about Covid, which many people, including the stale cheeto, wanted to blame China for. However, Covid is SARS, and if anyone recalls, SARS has been happening for about fifteen years. Maybe a little more, and we all used to see people with their masks on in other countries on TV. I think I remember seeing mostly Japanese people with masks. That was a long time ago. So I would say that is a virus that has been contained with extreme success and consideration. And I personally am grateful to face the virus with luxuries of Zoom and facebook and occasional instacart, and to have already gone through some good years where the economy was not shut down and I was able to travel for school. As obvious as God's care is in that, I will not hesitate to also show some gratitude to all the people in other countries who did the opposite of the biological warfare they were accused of. And I find it even ruder that people actually refused to discuss biological warfare anyway and went straight for the racism. Calling it "China virus" without deploying any armies or protection in a war. So it wasn't about biological warfare anyway and if it was, people were too cowardly to discuss it. How terrible, and war is actually something that should be legitimately prepared for anyway with extreme care for our diverse population where anyone could seem like an enemy under some conditions. And I go further with it than most and disagree with anyone who thinks that some privileged people somehow maintain their prosperity and safety with no attack. That view disgusts me and I don't see how anyone won't acknowledge the erosion and cultural assaults that are part of everyone's lives as we try to deal with overwhelming healthcare burdens, shark tech power hungry control freaks, unavoidable inappropriate media being force fed to everyone's kids, rates of autism with no residential or care provisions anywhere in

sight despite multiple multiple billionaires, a food supply that can't
be trusted and is replaced or even destroyed with no replacement by
greedy copycats who proudly hawk their aggressive harvest from
white flight to Portland and Seattle which continues to post a
disgusting symbolic green logo over the only thing that helped us
get through any of it besides our own supernatural strength that
some people didn't have because the expensive schools found it to
seem more intellectual to teach everyone that nothing's true. Who do
people want to be the victims? Who do people want to be the good
guys? Sometimes solutions are more obvious than people realize,
and the route to being a good person is surprisingly instant if that
was what people really wanted.

Glory to God, or Gloria Steinhem?

 Well, such good news about a one-shot covid vaccine except some articles have said that the vaccine development involved the use of aborted fetuses. But Johnson and Johnson insists that it was "just clones." Well that is reassuring. And okay obviously I don't know much about biology but if it is just cells you need then why is it from fetuses? I am just wondering if they are actually keeping fetuses "alive" in some sci-fi dystopian nightmare even worse than our other problems in this country that began attracting bad people to come here through pornography media many years ago. So now we know, which could be one of the purposes of why the pandemic happened, though of course I am not one of those people who thinks that hurricane katrina was a punishment for voodoo.

 Anyway, I will probably be thinking about this for a while, and grieving with a grief that yes, is actually worse than my grief for a virus that for most of us is sad but at least not a direct slap in the face to God and his people in our name or any name. Probably Big Pharma would also not want us to miss their celebrated and successful nailing of their truest targets, which is many or even most Covid heroes who just risked their lives with exhaustion and now have a dilemma of even keeping their jobs and are certainly legitimately persecuted if they are Christian or Catholic or just merely kept their moral compassion despite aggressive education efforts to convince people of a certain political supremacy that continues to be disguised as anti-racism defending poor ignorant "white"christians from themselves.

 I could see dismissing this issue entirely, and definitely support those who do, but it actually is a conundrum for me, because it is so obvious to me how even the most necessary articles about it are used to make Catholics and other good people seem weirdly fretful with some kind of hypocrit scrupulosity, all the while spreading alarming fear on purpose about the moral crisis of tainting something on this scale. Someone on facebook was quick, too, to mention the child abuse scandals in the Catholic church as soon as an article about this was posted. Her nasty addition to the discussion is more relevant than she realizes, for the opposite reason of the arrogance behind it, which is the way that issue too was used to smear the church's reputation instead of being seen in the context of a whole country where one in three children are abused. Gee, some of it was in church settings? Well we should all not believe in Jesus anymore and send more money to the northerners who are ashamed because they had to compromise everything faster than most other people as America's addictions caught up to us all. Now the dilemma can be for people in other countries who have to decide whether to accept help from the "wicked west."

I agree with the pope that people should feel free to get the vaccine anyway, but I do not plan to ignore the tragedy of disrespect to religious people that continues in this country. Just around the corner and for some people now within days or minutes, our real home in heaven is waiting, and no lies will be tolerated in the media there or in any hidden room where people think they have gotten away with a contemptuous racism against God and God only. This has to mean that there are a lot of people personally who won't be tolerated there either, and if you really want people to hate you, then try to warn people about that

whose photo is on your drivers license?

Well everyone, how are you doing. This is a normal worldly monk post like most of my old ones. And it is about the common teaching for people that their identity is "in Christ." And I just want to say that I think that as people try to use their gifts and help others, then some of their identity actually might be found in a more multi-faceted quality of who they are as they participate in life. So while it is good to not base things too much on other people's perceptions or success that can be taken away, if people keep seeking some undefinable thing called "identity" in God or "Christ," who in the end, is really his own self, then they might miss out on some ways of being that could have ironically been more beneficial in the long run. In fact, the more I have done the best I could in any way, the more I find that idea to be a cheap religious teaching that doesn't make that much sense, when so many people could be happier and fulfilled by investing in things that really bring them to life in a good way and cause a great harvest of almost anything. Are people saying that quote as a response to identity politics and racism? I think that a more actualizing achievement-based strategy could help with that too. People say, this is why you have lost everything in your life and God knows you held secret selfish ambitions. But I know that is not true and that most people have no idea what they mean when they tell everyone their identity is "in Christ" except to say please stop doing things well because at church our veiled message every time is that we are better than you.

dear liberal hypocrits,

Do you not think we see that for many of you,"social justice" is code for white slavery? Honestly to me it is a goal I can work with until it is turned into more blatant rape and trafficking, which has been a current in our culture already much too long for anyone to really believe that the cowardly power plays from media and government are any kind of new revolution. I am not fooled by bad people using black teens as human shields to advance the drug trade and jail waste that actually probably is the most effective strategy for destroying the so called fortresses of supposed "white power." But as this thinly disguised assault continues, there is another denial that paths to honest work for anyone are also disappearing as private and free industry is eaten from both the top and bottom by either corporate sharks with no accountability or socialist bums who think Colonel Bernie Sanders can save them from the health problems they opted for themselves though their insurance policy of trying to outlaw honest work and good behavior. Liberty and Justice are the keys to a system where society shares a collective pay-off, and the slavery that people really want will only be found when people do what they are supposed to along a path straight to heaven. The reward is compounding and eternal, and anyone can feast on the rewards with just a minimum of faith and the most reasonable and personalized portion of action that would follow. Don't think that you are accepted as some kind of ally for oppressed people while crowds of squawking time-wasters betray you by hiding the truth of salvation provided by God through Jesus Christ and his teaching. People who say it is not prosperous do not know what prosperity is. Who are your true friends? It might not be anyone from this world for a while, but the truth is destined to prevail in every moment and every case, and crime will never pay no matter how much it is snuck in to every day commerce or bludgeoned onto people more forcefully once everyone is frustrated to be busted for their lies, always exposed as the same old uncreative ploys of disrespect where bad people demand you pay for their mistakes.

hugging feet

Ok this blog post is more simple than some of the other posts and it has to do with the tradition of "footwashing" in the bible, usually associated with serving others because of the scene where Jesus washes his disciples feet and tells them that to be great you must be a servant. But I just want to share a little theory which is that I think there is something else about it that could really help people if they saw it, and I think it has to do with a love so great that people felt like kneeling at each other's feet, like bowing almost in a way that you can't do because it is so near to worship. And washing feet was the way to do that without crossing that line. I say that not based on biblical scholarship and anyone who has a problem with that can wash their own feet in the bathtub. But I say it from feeling a few times with just a number of people that if I saw them I would hug their feet because of what they did for me. It is often people like teachers, but not always, and ironically it is a love so great that I am mostly safe from turning it into some kind of idolatry. It is really something to think about not just in terms of when and why to do things like feet washing ceremonies, but to think of how to facilitate or promote that kind of love in your life or other people's lives. I think in our culture sometimes it has happened outside the church in workplaces or other social experiences where people can know each other that well and do something for each other that causes that kind of adoration. Anyway it is just something to keep in mind and I think it is a rare thing that shouldn't turn into a paranoia of suspecting there is not enough love to go around. The fact is that Jesus's life was a miracle so he had that kind of love almost all the time. Do you make that the goal or does it come from working with others for more specific goals? I do not know. I think God tells us to feed the poor and do justice for people not just for their sake but for us to have meaning and purpose that causes love. That is all I will say about it except that contrary to some feelings, it could be that more groveling is needed and not less for many people.

the pope's recent leadership

Ok, everyone, the pope just said some crazy stuff about not blessing gay marriage and I don't want to ruin anything but I will say that I think he has sufficiently cracked the code that gay marriages can in fact be blessed by God and not just that but caused by God, and the pope is doing something from Jesus's teaching where you hide your righteousness so as not to be praised by humans. I almost can't stand the intensity of that kind of sacrifice knowing the popularity and media celebration he could have had, but I will go ahead and mess up his plan a little by saying that I think a lot of people have figured out that there could be more variety to marriage that everyone realized for a while. And the gender variants that forced us to discover this don't have to be celebrated or despised or denied. I personally believe that marriage is usually designed as a gendered thing as opposed to friendship, and that is the very reason that gay marriage has to happen for some people, because their gender really is bent so to have a gendered relationship means being in something that seems like a "same sex" union to other people. But that is how they attained the gendered union because they really did feel more like the opposite gender. Is that really so complicated? For me it is, and becomes a constant source of torment when a whole society weighs in on it all. But some of the people who opted to give up religion due to societal foibles ended up truthful and free and won't lose that reward from God. And I think the pope knows it and supports people in a good way and I think his little reputation sacrifice is a bit much when he and Pope Benedict to me are already the best popes ever!! Way to go fellas! A faithful pope for the Catholics and a secret nonpope for the Protestants! It's genius! So who does that leave for the Orthodox? I would say Oprah but it's not my choice. Well that is all everyone, have a great day!

My 2 Cents on Government Spending

 A post today is simple which is that I agree it is a good time for reparitions. People could think that the economic losses should cause people to wait, but it is all the more reason and all the more appropriate for people to give from their poverty when they can. That is what black people were forced to do for generations, to find resources from nowhere and live anyway without basic needs. So it is just the right priority during Covid recovery. We should tax ourselves voluntarily and as a country and as local communities. Many people are already doing the work. I expect to do most of my part during purgatory and think it will be good. I do not plan to pay back the suffering as a punishment but instead will take Christ's offer of all you can eat forgiveness while I learn to cook all you can eat restaurant food. I am also going to live at the mall for a while and run a surprise store with things that can only be sold in purgatory. That is all for today and now I will try to work on imaginary mice novels. I owe a 40 dollar pledge to holocaust survivors but will probably still also buy cupcakes for myself on credit.

you have heard it said

So a new idea I have is that instead of saying "God loves me," I could think "God has a variety of feelings towards me." I think theologians figured out a long time ago that all those feelings would be some form of love if I am right with him through Christ, but it could be beneficial in some way to entertain a thought that there first of all could be a range in how happy he is with my behavior at any given time, and that he invented time for a reason that involves his participation as well. So people say God can see everything at one time and forgives me anyway, but if I am supposed to do things like count the clock during history class or grow up or try to do what I am supposed to throughout a day that includes responsibilities involving other days, then I could spend some of that time guessing that God might have a complex emotional reaction perpetually matching my status in creation at any given time so that he is literally not wasting "time." As in, he is not wasting the concept and creation of time that he invented possibly as a facilitation not at all of something linear or one dimensional or even glowing blob-like circular but to cause variety that would then include his own perception of all his people. And if it takes a lot of people to entertain him in just the right way, maybe it takes a lot of interesting things about each person and their life like maybe even bad and good for all the complete reactions to happen. Like God does not want to be bored, so sometimes he is mad, happy, and sad instead of just doing miracles all the time. To me it would help if there was something in the Bible to back that up like if there were stories of him doing things like being a carpenter or something. Then we would know not to just tell people God loves them when really we are supposed to say something like "I wonder if the way you just juggled pies and then threw one in someone's face reminds God of the time that he invented dinosaurs." That is probably how poetry got started unless the Bible says something different like if it said "In the beginning God was speechless." It actually says the opposite which is very interesting because it did seem kind of quiet and dark

early on, not in an agnostic or atheistic kind of way but more like a roaring vacuum which is interesting to think about like instead of an explosion moving outward, God calling things from outward towards him and everything appearing from nowhere in the opposite direction. Think about it and it could correct another idea of it to land in some middle ground that matches the Genesis account that I actually think has more clues about existence than people realize.
 But I think the science happens all over the Bible so people can't cheat and zoom in to the part they think has the technology breakthrough they are looking for. I myself think there is a hidden parenting manual across all the books of the Bible where God is three years old during the time of Noah, twelve years old when David says the battle belongs to the Lord, a teenager in Ezekiel, a young adult getting married in the gospels, a middle aged person in the letters of Paul, and then 70 years old in the book of Revelation which actually descibes him as having white hair and bronze feet.
 Like that is kind of weird like a Florida retirement kind of thing, not to criticize anyone but if you see it like that you probably could find some cures for some diseases too, or a good recipe for fish, or the story of western civilization.

Swivel Chair Mahem

Hi everyone, I hope you are having a good day. I got a new cot and am having fewer hallucinations and more sleep. So that is good. I had to take some anxiety medicine and whenever I do, I think of people who have anxiety and don't believe in or know about psychiatric medicine and I feel sad for them because literally you can't breathe without anxiety medicine sometimes. That is why I think the religion problems in this country need to be addressed and the persecution of ignorant sad people from those more educated or just differently educated is not helping anyone. Anyway that is not the main thing I am writing about today. The main thing I am here to discuss is which swivel chair should I try to order once I get the stimulus check for 1400 dollars. For just part of that cash, I am thinking of buying one of these chairs for my newly cleared out apartment which I can also move to another location if I get approved for a housing situation designed for mentally ill people. I have high hopes for that and think that it will help me survive in NYC for a while longer and work as a peer counselor. I think I might try to get the green chair because it is more affordable or the yellow chair because it is on sale and might not be available later on. And it could be that in a new apartment I could try to collect all four eventually. Task chairs online start at about 60 dollars and go to a range of about $150 for a nice cool one and then higher than that for some that are almost like recliners and can cost up to 800 dollars. That is a bit much for me but I think the idea of an upholstered swivel chair is great and can also be a way to sit low to the ground which I find to be comforting. Anyway in some cultures people pay you to sit in a swivel chair and do work, but I have found myself to have drifted towards laying on a cot and talking to imaginary mice and rabbits. So that is the new task is to figure out what to do about that. Get it? "task," like "task chair." It is worth googling and can be so fun to see all the designs. Well have a great day everyone. This blog post reminds me of William Cowper's famous poem called "the Task."

please call me st. faggotcrap when you canonize me

Well everyone, it is Thursday afternoon. Apparently everyone on twitter was told to denounce "Asian hate." I agree except for the fact that I suspect it is just more marching orders from the satanic media control that's really targeting religious people, especially whites or anyone who identifies with a previous form of America. It's also probably prep work for Kamala, which is likely to include plans for a convenient Biden assassination as soon as possible or just as soon as believable. Maybe it will be an inside job, or maybe they will provoke Russia on purpose where Putin likes to poison people. I doubt Obama will be the one to do it but whatever happens I am sure will be exactly as non-shocking as having the piece of white cardboard for president in the first place. A piece of blank poster board is kind of appropriate to represent the half-nation of protesters that borrowed some old-school democrat sincerity and mixed it with a new rabid hatred and anti-white racism towards people who pay taxes and hold on to old fashion notions of citizenship. I think the United States should take the cue to go ahead and break up so that not everyone can be so easily targeted at one time. People can do what they want, but from what I see in New York, the liberal sharks and worse are on the way for everyone's children, which they would eat with a knife and fork if they were more civilized, but at this point only know how to rape and humiliate with bad music, dishonest curriculums, and kidnapping from foreign rapist drug dealers who fell into that work from failing to bomb Israel like Biden wants to do.

General Tso has been nothing but nice to me

Hi everyone, the secret messages are telling me to do another blog post to reassure everyone that I will take my psychiatric medicine later. Of course I will everyone. Don't say you were at the insurrection if you weren't really there. Anyway I am about to go try to get some cash and then go get some Chinese food, which honestly could be a little bit awkward because it could seem like I am just stopping by because of the StopAsianHate campaign. And maybe it will be taken as a gesture of politics but really I just like Chinese food and feel that my gallbladder can handle it after months of causing me to honestly not be even a minimally good neighbor during Covid for one of my favorite restaurants called Panda House. Surely I could have ordered the dumplings a few more times or some wonton soup. I should definitely turn myself in to the authorities at CNN for that but so far will just plan to order the hot and sour soup, crab rangoons, and a certain kind of chicken that is probably not in network for my health insurance.

Anyway I will also pass along a little joke from my friend who has cancer, which is that my friend said her medical people explained that she is "eating for two" now: herself and the cancer. I think there could have been a better way to frame that but my friend really wanted me to have that joke for free so of course I will mention it for all my readers which actually probably even at this time includes some nice helpful people as well as legal sharks from Barnes and Noble who may soon be as excited as anyone else when I announce to everyone that I have hidden three hundred dollars in several random books at each Barnes and Noble in America. Do you guys get that? It is like telling people to go rummage messily through all the books on the shelves, kind of like all the customers always do anyway. Well have a great day everyone, please take everything I say with a grain of salt and hopefully no MSG.

Wait for it...

Ok I wrote another installment of the Barnes and Noble "chain" of events which I am keeping to myself for now and will add to the book I am working on and possibly post later this week. I am also waiting a while to post a very shocking description of a book online where I talk about a bloody axe for child abusers. It seems that I have three very fruitful and honorable missions in my life which is writing, the conspiracy, and being tortured on personal and societal levels. I am not alone in any of it and the missing readership that I haven't been able to account for is probably comprised of young people from a different generation who will appreciate having a unique blessing reserved for them. And I guess that is why people have been saying that the other stuff should be enough for all of us now and that I am the one who had enough to go on and should never have complained. I can kind of see it but think that the torture dynamic actually is based on a truly un-rightful loss experience of an actual specific reader audience and earnings being with-held unfairly. So it could be an ironic creative circumstance that took a lot of thought and effort to maintain, but mostly I think that for me to be genuine in any of it means expressing my true opposition to the injustice involved. And if people want to say some of that injustice is from me then I can kind of work with that but think that filter just increases the ever-expanding loss that should never have happened. So maybe all three things were not meant to be anyway, and the writing was supposed to be advertising and the conspiracy was supposed to be overt youth ministry and the torture was supposed to be other people's kind acceptance of the public faith I shared. So all those chronic errors would account for the frustrating feeling of failure and grief. But I could be wrong about that grouping and the conspiracy of helpful people might not appreciate being part of a trinity that includes criminal torture. But that is what I feel from the church as a consistent consensus is that I am supposed to be overjoyed whenever I am reduced to a forgiveness machine meant only to experience pain and loss for no reason. But they are saying it is pain and loss and meaninglessness for a reason, and once you get to the opportunity to forgive, then you have it made, so don't be a fool, or at least be a fool in the right way which is through love and kindness. Well that is fine for today and I will keep the other thoughts to myself. Is that what everyone wanted? To not hear the juicy facts of the matter? That is the phrase I could not remember yesterday. So as my memory fails people will have no explanation for why they will not be as much of a gameshow contestant as originally hoped for in my prayer system that unfortunately does not support or reward the kind of abuse I am expected to tolerate even at this very moment where miracles are disappearing down a funnel to the basement of never never land where someone I liked is about to be informed that the deal is off if certain choices were made. I hate all of you and wish that I was never born.

If you're reading this, i have made my decision to drink three coffees today

Ok everyone, I got some sleep. I feel better and am going to go outside and go to the store in my neighborhood. I think I will buy my pet guinea pig an apple at the store and some new better pet food. I thought of something to say when people are mean to me when I walk down the street. When the bad people in my neighborhood make dog noises at me or jangle their keys or whatever and block me on the sidewalk as I try to get to the grocery store, instead of cursing I am going to say back to them "Bad Dog, Brandy," like we used to say to my dog when she chewed up the walls of our house. And I will say "Do you need to go out?" and anything else I can think of. I think that will be virtually untraceable instead of the criminal harassment that the bad people are trying to provoke. Some of them are probably from my old social work school or the socialists who send me emails saying I went to certain meetings when I do not even know those people. My name is on those lists from signing a rent freeze petition during Covid, which I do think would have been a good idea. Anyway I guess the conspiracy decided that a decline in my behavior and functioning would either be an interesting part of my writing later on or just a good way for me to die senselessly after a lifetime of effort to do anything meaningful whatsoever. You just have to learn to change your goals along the way. Think, okay, in my heart I want to write poems, but that is a decoy for the real goal of education which is brain damage. I mean am I right? They should say it as a learning objective like I used to include the idea of teachers showing care for young people on my extra paperwork as a teacher. I think that is why I got persecuted, but the secret messages are telling me only Christ got persecuted. I kind of get it but kind of think that most people are better off finding some middle ground in their minds and going ahead with some life that isn't a perpetual heresy trial but instead appears almost normal to other neighbors. That is why I stoop to other people's level, which by certain logic applied to me is an ascent anyway isn't it? Like the logic that we all at heart deserve torture? Well I feel that is applied to me as a recipient but not as someone on the other side of it, when other people seem to have gotten a green light on their abuse from somewhere. Anyway I will definitely try to lighten up with these posts but I kind of thought pretending to be a war veteran was a way of joking about the unjokable.

Good Afternoon, Vietnam.

I think I have several topics for another whole batch of blog posts, but instead of waiting for the inspiration that is probably from my seizure disorder anyway, I will try to say it all in one post about fun memories from life at Barnes and Noble for twelve years. Here is a passport photo I got in May 1999 when I thought I was about to be on a summer staff for overseas mission trips all summer. I did need to do that but could not because of manic episodes. But as it fell through and life turned into a series of tricks and emotional torment, I had already seen the path before me in my mind and knew that I was doing what I was supposed to. I went to work at Barnes and Noble in October and stayed there for twelve years to become a poet. I am thankful even though the bookstore job gave me permanent brain damage and I now call people names in my poems and essays. Here is the passport photo.

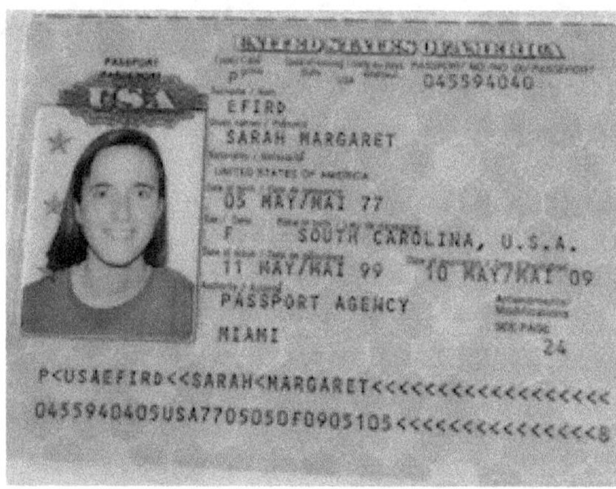

Here is my recent veteran photo from after coming home from Nam:

I have stopped being heavy handed with the word "torture" and am moving on to a new phase of recovery where I try to be patient and forgive and keep things to my self sometimes instead of trying to get whatever credit would make up for what has been lost through treatment and mistreatment that got combined. Recently the conspiracy and some church people from the same brand as the mission trip organization helped me defeat a cluster of enemy demonic authorities that may have been part of the more personalized failure and spiritual abuse I have suffered. I think I won't share the whole story but in my mind recently decided to be more accepting and forgiving in the old ways that I was taught, and I changed the presbyterian hymn asking for consecration and sang the thoughts, take my life and let it be, desecrated lord to thee. I think that was God's behavior goal for me, fitting for what he has provided, and right after that attitude adjustment, I saw what looked like a hologram image of: *"Prince, a guy yelling and I heard the voice but don't know what it said, a demon named Torture, a light skinned female with no visible head and tattoos of words written all over her stomach, a guy who looks like that drug dealer in my neighborhood, and then a twitch. Then I heard voices say things like*

I think that it could have to do with me getting my second Covid shot on April 1st.

People say I could still keep this stuff to myself and many psychics probably do all the time for religious reasons, but for me, it is something so valuable for anyone to learn from so I have decided to tell all about it. And I think that "hypergraphia" might come with epilepsy for the very reason that these backstage passes to what is happening to all of us should not be wasted.

Probably you all see how this writing could be divided into posts for several blogs but I think this is all for now. I just want to say that I think that even if my soul and life is what is infested with these evil spirits or authorities or worse, that my new theory is any of us can be used as "perches" for these things to attack other people, either through our speech, our actions and participation in bad things, or even silent misperception that adds to a loss people don't realize until it has happened. But anyway God knows that a lot of people have helped me, and he knows that many people have gone through worse things and done better. But he also seems to have a plan for people to learn about his ways from someone who could be counted on to be an interesting mix of good and bad all the time. I guess everyone is like that, but I really wanted attention and said so, and God apparently felt that a war on my soul could serve as a comforting reflection of what others have gone through too. So I am happy to share about it and let people think what they want. I saw a skull again a few minutes ago which I think has to do with when Dr. Brown abused me at scoliosis appointments when I was 14 years old. Every problem has a way of exposing other problems if we let it, so we should all tell the truth and forgive each other because a lot of stuff will be sorted out later and the greatest rewards come from faith, most of all in what God has shared in the life and death of JC Macgillagoo of Shropshire, also known as the root of Jesse, rose of

Sharon, wonderful counselor, prince of peace, man of sorrows,
acquainted with grief, smitten by God, and afflicted, pierced for our
transgressions, crushed for our iniquities.
He was oppressed, and he was afflicted,
    yet he opened not his mouth;
like a lamb that is led to the slaughter,
    and like a sheep that before its shearers is silent,
    so he opened not his mouth.
8 By oppression and judgment he was taken away;
    and as for his generation, who considered
that he was cut off out of the land of the living,
    stricken for the transgression of my people?
9 And they made his grave with the wicked
    and with a rich man in his death,
although he had done no violence,
    and there was no deceit in his mouth.

10 that at the name of Jesus every knee should bow, of those in
heaven, and of those on earth, and of those under the
earth, 11 and that every tongue should confess that Jesus
Christ is Lord, to the glory of God the Father.

I mixed up a lot of verses for that in my usual way, on the verge in
some eyes as not caring at all, but if people wanted me to do better
then they should have included me the right way in the first place
instead of throwing me in a snake pit for what will end up being my
entire life. Do people wear camouflage among civilians? Do bad
people hide in good places? Why would corporate sharks visit my
church to use sermons against me? Thank you Matt, thank you Bill.
Thank you Barnes and Noble customers for putting yourselves in
front of the most accurate video cameras of all time, which is the
eyes of God as you either give him your life or side with snakes at
the Borders, or in the Nile, or Amazon.

email to self

my blog is fine. i am cleaning it up for possible visitors but who cares. it has been five years of blogging and it seems that the books are all going to remain as ebooks. that is fine with me. i think that is a good idea.

not even guinea pig in the sky needs to be in print. who really cares anyway. the loss has already happened.

those books were for a time and a market that is gone now.

people just watched me write along, knowing it was for no reason at all except to experience an extra range of emotional abuse that has enlisted the innocent help from hundreds of people who did care. and they comforted me but little did they know that all their support was hijacked for a cruel trick.

the worst of the barnes and noble thing that i remember from being in the music department was in fact contrived, and i have to say that i can kind of see barnes and noble's exasperation of that kind of crap. i had a lot of potential to help people and now i am just a lazy pig who curses a lot.

anyway thanks everyone for all the help. it is all for no reason except for some human concept of glory that a bunch of bored religious people think they understand well enough to justify ruining and wasting someone's actualized potential in exchange for some kind of demonstration of patience that they think is the whole point but will actually put me in an outrageous status of showing up on judgement day and finding out that I should have killed myself a long time ago and once i chose to stay alive, the wrongs were so bad that I should have killed several thousand people but let the guilty go free in the wrong way as described in proverbs. for me to show up after all this crap and find out that i was supposed to be an axe murderer based on how i was treated is a problem that seems a little bit too bad to be traced back just to me.

and i would say that if anyone had any say in it then it is pretty bad ministry and my consolation will probably be seeing for myself on judgement day how God deals with incompetent losers who interfere in the lives of people already enough on track.

that is not even all i have to say but i think that this path of printing these books and letting the other stuff be journal material is a wise choice for now.

but honestly at some point i do think some of us can say that staying alive and using any amount of wisdom or virtue for any reason whatsoever is an egregious example of throwing our pearls to pigs. not necessarily because everyone is bad, but because people did not succeed in destroying those snatching up everyone's blessings as they almost happen.

and to me, for my blog and books to be filled with mad lashes while still knowing that i have used a lot of self control to not say worse things for ten whole years now, is really all the reason to change careers, and start a new writing career that is basically just hate speech in all forms for all people.

journal

You guys think the abuse and swindling that continues after twenty years is an opportunity I should not throw away and that I should be happy about every day that passes by without a harvest from five careers worth of labor, but I think you are all very wrong with consequences that have already affected thousands and millions of people who could have been well on their way with safe and productive paths of faith. I escaped religious communities where people hyper-managed their own moods as a fruitless and small pursuit of righteousness and I learned to get stuff done that would actually help people. And I was patient with a lot of outrageous ignorance and mistreatment along the entire way, and God delivered with absolute miracles. But people still insist that the goal of my existence is to somehow keep producing some personal attitude of forgiveness while watching my whole culture and world flail around like idiots and dig themselves deeper into a debt that will be reckoned with to the penny. And now a more minor social debt and financial debt has accumulated for me personally after saving and living by self control on a level that may not have ever occurred before in this world and includes my own parent's savings now too which is where I learned the absurd and harsh frugality. I hope everyone's share of the tragic mockery will be a clue as to what I have had to tolerate in my constantly and deliberately toxified and muddied life, ruined in automatically updated ways upon every breakthrough by a consensus of reptile people who simply can't support a person who does what they are supposed to. Everything in my life turns to false hope, and if church people want to say, yes, that is exactly what we tried to tell you, then all I can wonder is why other people like me aren't also on disability with no job prospects except to endure further tests of patience from each new roll out of hardship that is either cruelly novel or insultingly the same old traps from everyone whose job in life is to count the money they stole from you. To me suicide is an obvious solution that I will still publicly entertain as the unfair but most supported option available, and as a harvest of death that the people in power insisted on no matter what random claims of other beliefs they hid behind while thinking no one sees the robbery, snobbery, and hobbylobbery.

Suicide Note Oct 23, 2020

Well everyone I am tired of people ruining my life. I have asked people to stop bothering me on purpose many times. I have done everything I could but somehow I still end up begging from my parents and being in debt and having to put up with emotional abuse in almost every environment I find myself in.

Church sucks, my neighborhood is racist and harasses me every day. My mental health care people gave me false hope about housing and have not successfully reported the barnes and noble crime.

My dad used me as my mom's replacement spouse against my will while she caused permanent damage to my whole mind and life.

The only job I was able to keep reliably was a source of constant torture and humiliation even though I was nice to every single employee and talked to every customer as a worthy person without a hint of acting or fakeness.

I tell the truth and do what I am supposed to pretty much all the time yet I am harassed and accused and hounded by intimidation from legal garbage more powerful than me.

I felt so happy to have a conspiracy giving me attention but it has betrayed me and turned me into an angry bad Christian who has lost reward after reward and wasted my opportunities because of a patience that was spent on enduring abuse from bad people.

I paid to have worthwhile activities through education but ended up with a nasty political environment that reinforces the lessons that the rest of our bad society has taught me which is nothing I do is ever good enough and it would have been better to not be born.

My life is reduced to that offensive conclusion which can serve only in a positive way as a last defense for the baby killers who think everything should revolve around them and their abortion habit that they expect innocent people like me to pay for.

That is why I am going to kill myself by March of next year. It is probably too late for anyone to do anything about it.

I will add a definite and irrevocable goodbye to the person I liked and held out for for several years. It seemed that the person scrogged a faggot from the community where I knew that person and I think the faggot knew the person was my person and should be considered to be as bad as a person can be and not be allowed to have a social work license.

I hereby reject my own license on the basis that the profession is too corrupt with bad philosophy, dishonest insurance, and hypocritical racism.

Some elementary school friends were nice to me and some other nice people along the way and I hope to see some people again in heaven but actually can only feel hopeful if I would essentially be starting over with a better country and people.

This note is probably what NYU wanted, but I wanted to be a good and productive person with enough love to survive. I do not have that and it is too late for anyone who was a prospect while people tortured me and did not succeed in securing a stable independence where I could be safe from not just current emotional abuse but the abuse that I successfully fled from.

Y'all's judgment day is your problem.
Signed, sarah efird

"kind of like CS Lewis but a homicidal maniac"

That is what a New York Times review could have been for my books, couldn't it. Maybe ten years ago, or 8, or 6, or 5, when I just decided to do the e-books, or maybe during the Trump years, but then probably Bernie would have won the election. I guess it all worked out fine and I should not interpret the continuing silence as not being somehow in my favor. I voted for Jo Jorgensen. Is that it? Because my life did not revolve around Trump? Because I had to stop volunteering places in case the FBI helping with the torture case saw the immigrants I was giving food to? I always search for the reasons behind my kaleidoscope of humiliation and rejection experiences. To what do I owe the honor of being the emotional abuse connoisseur that I am? By now it could be a lot of things. The smell on my clothes from my apartment that's a mix of bug spray, rotten groceries, and dirty socks, or maybe hitting myself on zoom meetings when the liberals change the filter to make me look worse because of privilege, or possibly the thing I keep living for, which is to stay alive when I don't want to. The irony of it I guess just ends up beating people at their own brand of comedy, which consists of calling me names while I walk down the street in my neighborhood, or newspaper articles from rich northerners calling evangelicals bullies. A gleeful crowd who made politics their religion can't wait to see Jesus Christ vengefully turn people like Michael Moore and Bill Maher into saints on Judgement Day in my face and everyone's face that has already been ground into the layer of dirt and dog crap all over our ruined country. Maybe people suspect me of being a cop because I care about child abuse, and they are trying to defund me before I get away with sharing any poems that tell teenagers not to rape people. I am sure everyone meant well and will not feel the same feelings of insult that makes me think of choosing a different heaven when I die, far from this society, abandoning many people who did support me and watched in horror as my absence was celebrated instead of some very funny Christian poetry that could have helped all the kids who had to face a pandemic without basic fundamentals about heaven, hell, and their future as slaves being trafficked overseas to Isis.

What if the horse at Armageddon turns out to be Mr. Ed

Well everyone, I have decided to shut down all my blogs, so this is my final mad blog post for a while. I thought of a few issues I could end with but I think I am just saying this is all for now before I share posts that are too charged and too… right about all the problems so much that readers start a war. That has been a surprise to me to see a new perspective from myself that is no longer trying to work things out with people different from me or helping others do the same but instead is an extreme reaction to outrageous abuse as I draw the line in my acceptance of absolute injustice presented as the salvation that people continue to turn down like fools. Anyway, every time I write I can see years' worth of material ahead of me but really think I am better off just working it out on my own instead of crowning a fifteen year writing span of jokes with white hot rage and a drooling, rabid counterattack like the animal that my society drove me to be. That is how my writing always sounds now. It could be a new genre. Let's remember that there is a conspiracy and people snuck me all the attention I could ever want and helped each other share their food, too. And the people I have complained about in recent blog posts were all in on it completely, so maybe they deserve either the benefit of the doubt, or at least my last few drops of patience as I finish my mental illness adventure and spiritual deterioration into one of those street prophets who talks about Judgement Day all the time. Other people know exactly the transition that has happened, and it is not in our hands anyway as our vigilant, life-long fears for our neighbors' doom turns onto complete agreement at their destruction.

Final Posts

Well everyone, I am ending all my blogs, but probably not my life, even though people made me feel that way on purpose for now about the twentieth year in a row. My reaction to people's abuse and consistent oppression strategies is pretty much the accurate disgust that people would guess it to be, though it seems that some people erroneously think God sees them differently. There is a growing hypocrisy in the north that started a long time ago, where everyone was told that anything anyone believes is equally true, and then equally not true, so don't bother, and now the new phase is to replace the lost faith and truth with a trio of socialism, buddhism, and racism. Some innocence mixed in dilutes the destructive power, but not enough. And speaking of power, the expectation seems to be that the ignorant south will just be dragged along like the dog tied to the car in the lampoon vacation movie. But I am not sure how many people will put up with it. I will die probably within just a few years and essentially be starting over with less than if I had never lived at all, but there is some spiritual lesson in that which I will eventually understand instead of a life's worth of glorious truth which was very common for people to experience for many years of the civilization that people are now turning against. Anyway, I feel that I could just keep writing for several years to express this exact shock and dismay in many forms as the same odd brand of blame and abuse accumulates all around me, mostly from the same people using the same hypocritical strategies but pretending to be revolutionary and defending the so-called victims of people who generally do what they are supposed to. But I am going to finish these blogs now instead of trying to keep up with every slight, and every worse-than-slight, which everyone will already be aware of on some level no matter what they decide to say in their continued satanic media assault.

Mental Health Post

I have found that a good way to assess your mental health status as compared to some kind of idea of normalcy is to think about what most people would have to go through to feel as bad as you feel. And for mentally ill people, it is often something like, they would have to run over their own dog in the drive way and then give a speech naked in front of their church and forced to eat the dog guts before then being attacked on video. And people might say, Gosh, that is sick, but really it is sick when people feel that bad every moment for years at a time and yet are treated worse in life every day and punished for it. So some of those same people show up at church or work and get told that they should stop complaining until they have real problems like cancer or grief. That right there is something for everyone to grieve about because it is a historical loss for the country and church that many people had to put up with that. But anyway on a personal note I am going to the hospital soon and am going to tell them that Nancy Pelosi authorized my euthanization.

Young Life Essay

So what went wrong with me and Young Life. It is something for anyone in churches and Christian ministries to learn from. The thing I am going to say is the solution is actually something that I was far beyond, and that is to include anyone at any level by facilitating the opportunity for them to simply share their testimony.

I say I was beyond this because I do think I successfully made friends with kids, showed care, and bore the responsibility well to come through on both the things I had a talent for and the things that were more difficult for me. I was good at giving talks, and if they had even remotely played to my strength in the most basic considerate way, I probably would have had a feeling of success instead of complete rejection from God and eventually worthlessness as a person. But Young Life ended up steering me more toward the things I would look stupid at, especially once we got a new team leader who needed to bond with people and apparently did so with me as a shield. There is no need to describe all of it, but I know now after a hard life what the reason was for stuff like the dorf skit and the final winter club where I had prepared a game and then was introduced as doing something completely unknown to me. The goal was for me to feel a final feeling of embarrassment and failure, maybe in front of everyone as a demonstration of Christian sacrifice, but no doubt also as a deliberate way to make that event be my last. Combined with a professor that semester telling my media arts class that Christians aren't creative and I personally was exactly the type of individual responsible for all the atrocities in the world, including the holocaust, there was no other possible outcome than for me to be suicidal, and therefore in my own eyes at least temporarily unfit for youth ministry.

Well that meant losing the supportive social scene that happened to be the exact reason why I felt able to attend an actually pretty nasty state school where they prided themselves on making people feel stupid for being from South Carolina. South Carolina, as in the University of South Carolina, home and home only to cheap studies about Darwin and Freud, three times removed and reduced to be aggressive agenda-driven material for inappropriate innuendos and jokes about how much they knew what we all really wanted was beer.

The Journalism school did pretty well, though, because they weren't academics, and my advertising professors saved my life at the same rate the church people lost faith in me and lost my faith for me as a service of their adherence to their own theological suspicions about gender-- specifically, my confused gender.

Back to the point, though, of these social tricks where people engineer things instead of helping people tell the truth and offer basic normal inclusion that doesn't victimize anyone. I want to say that something very interesting about my mental breakdown during sophomore year, extremely connected to a spiritual crisis that in retrospect probably could have and should have been prevented, was how much it probably wasn't all because of my gender problems. I think that's part of it, but the thing that really might be more universal is something that we should all guard each other's hearts from. Young Life often liked to highlight some of its cooler people, and not necessarily for totally bad reasons. It's not a game to be reaching out to high school students who did not grow up with automatic church, and there is definitely a call for navy seals of popularity. But when you have someone like me, who was half nerd and half cool, people all the time see a chance to take someone down who would otherwise be a challenge or a rival for acceptance. People actually like cool nerds, and like to be cool nerds, and that is because at heart, everyone is a cool nerd. People have strengths and weaknesses and things that make them different and things that make them relate. Everyone should play to their strengths and overcome their weaknesses.

The theme for leaders that year was "Mission Possible," but it was exactly that rewarding feeling of fulfilled goals that was so lacking for me and probably withheld on purpose or at the very least neglectfully unfacilitated. And yes it is reasonable to expect adult provision of emotional safety when you are an 18-year-old volunteer.

I feel a little bit bratty and stupid to be even re-visiting the topic now 25 years later, but that's after enduring my entire adulthood without the mental health that somehow disappeared at the exact rate that I got in my car every week at 5 am to go lead Bible studies in college. All I could really think of to say was that Jesus told people they were the light of the world and the salt of the earth. And what does salt do? Well I will tell you what it does. It kills slugs. What does light do? It helps you see the slugs. If that' s not good enough Christian ministry for people in South Carolina, then some people might be in the wrong state. A state such as a sinful state of total depravity.

Anyway, you all see where I am going with this, which is now to purgatory where I can try again to find meaningful work and love, evolving as I should towards heaven and not towards the hell of USC's parking lot, where they do nothing but take back your scholarship through parking tickets.

Refried Bean lives in New York City
and is learning how to be a peer counselor.
Refried has one guinea pig left named Dave.